INSIDE THE ARAB REVOLUTION

Three Years on the Front Line of the Arab Spring

Koert Debeuf

INSIDE THE ARAB REVOLUTION

Three Years on the Front Line of the Arab Spring

Foreword by Guy Verhofstadt: A Mediterranean Community

Second edition: january 2015

D/2014/45/263 - ISBN 978 94 014 1824 9 – NUR 697/692/754

Cover design: Frisco
Interior design: theSWitch

© Koert Debeuf and Lannoo Publishers nv, Tielt, 2014.

LannooCampus Publishers is a subsidiary of Lannoo Publishers,
the book and multimedia division of Lannoo Publishers nv.

All rights reserved.
No part of this publication may be reproduced and/or
made public, by means of printing, photocopying,
microfilm or any other means, without
the prior written permission of the publisher.

LannooCampus Publishers
Erasme Ruelensvest 179, box 101
3001 Leuven | Belgium
www.lannoocampus.be

Acknowledgements

There is a long list of people without whom this book would not exist. During the three years I was the representative of the Alliance of Liberals and Democrats for Europe (ALDE) in the Arab world hundreds if not thousands of people contributed to my mission in one way or another. First of all, I have to thank the Members of Parliament of the ALDE group and the ALDE secretariat, who made this mission possible. As it is a mission unique in its kind, they applied courage and all manner of creativity to make it happen. I also appreciated their concern and support when, time and again, I exposed myself to danger in Egypt and Syria.

I would also like to express my gratitude and appreciation to those Arab leaders for the confidence they have given to my work and that of ALDE: Amr Moussa, Mahmud Jibril, Ahmad Hariri, Salim Idriss, Awn Khasawneh, Naguib Al Masri, Yassine Brahim, Fawaz Tello as well as their advisors Mohamed Madkour, Haithem Elkeeb, Khalil Choucair, Rabih Fakhredinne, Samah Atout and Riadh Mouakhar. All were a treasure of information and important catalysts for action.

A warm thanks to the many European and Arab friends who provided me with an intellectual and emotional oasis in times of madness and destruction in the Arab world. Here too the list is long, but special mention must go to Stephan Neetens, Jorn De Cock, Yaser Al Zayat, Rasha Kamel, Mona Eltahawy, Tarik Salama, Tamer Fouad, Bassem Sabry, Mahmud Salem, Marwa Maamoon, Hazem Amin, Rami Jarrah, Deiaa Dughmoch and Sultan Al Qassemi.

This book would not have been possible without my publisher, Gert De Nutte of Lannoo Campus. He worked very quickly and efficiently in order to realise this project and did so enthusiastically. The *EUObserver* too was crucial to my mission and this book. They gave me the opportunity to write blog posts that reached a wide European audience.

I don't know where to start with thanking Guy Verhofstadt. He gave me the opportunity to work as an advisor on his cabinet in 2003 when he was prime minister. I was only 28 years old. I was his speechwriter, liaison officer at the Belgian parliament, political advisor and later, spokesperson. He appointed me director of a new think tank at Open Vld, the Flemish liberal party, and his chief of staff when he became the president of the ALDE group. Without his conviction, activism and support my mission to the Arab world would not have happened; nor would it have succeeded. It is a great honour to work for one of the most extraordinary politicians in Europe.

Finally, words cannot express my gratitude to my family. My wife, Renilde Knevels, and my daughters, Charlotte and Louise, took the tough decision to drop everything and join me on this unpredictable adventure. They started a new life in Cairo, a challenging city to live in. Not once did they complain as I headed out on dangerous trips. My parents have often asked me if I truly realise how indispensible my wife's support has been. They don't have to worry...

Table of content

I. Foreword by Guy Verhofstadt: A Mediterranean Community. A New Vision for the European Southern Neighbourhood	13

II. This Is an Arab Revolution	27
Atlantic centrism	30
Is Cairo the next New York?	35
More than an Arab Spring	37
A tsunami of change	39
The Arab versus the French Revolution	40

III. Inside the Arab Revolution. Three Years of Publishing	61
Egypt. Reflections from October 2011 to September 2013	**67**
1. There is no problem with the Copts…	69
2. Towards a second Egyptian revolution	71
3. In bitter fight, Egyptian Islamists rig the elections	73
4. From Twitter Revolution to Twitter Democracy	75
5. Are the Muslim Brothers Muslim Republicans?	77
6. Elections in Egypt: some early conclusions	80
7. How to safeguard the revolution in Egypt: an outsider's perspective	84
8. Out of the crisis with an Egyptian triumvirate? An outsider's perspective	86
9. President Morsi: cooperating or disappearing?	88
10. Morsi is a blessing for Egyptian liberals: an outsider's perspective	91
11. Belgium: unconstitutional parliament for 10 years and still rolling!	94
12. Egypt and the psychology of dictatorship: an outsider's perspective	96
13. To safeguard democracy in Egypt, postpone the referendum: an outsider's perspective	100

14. The suicide mission of the Muslim Brotherhood: an outsider's perspective … 103
15. And now, the end is near for President Morsi … 107
16. Egypt: will there be order after the chaos? An outsider's perspective … 110
17. How President Morsi ousted himself: a too short overview … 113
18. What should the EU decide on Egypt? … 123

Tunisia. Some reflections … 129
1. Political fight for power in Egypt and Tunisia … 131

Syria. Reflections from May 2012 to January 2014 … 137
1. Syria is a second Bosnia. Assad is Milosevic … 140
2. Eyewitness account – Syria: a report from the field … 143
3. Syrian insurgents say aid isn't getting where it needs to go (Article New York Times) … 149
4. The Free Syrian Army does exist and is growing stronger by the day by Koert Debeuf & Response by Aron Lund … 155
5. What does the Free Syrian Army want? … 165
6. Not the jihadists but we are the problem … 168
7. We never learn: Syrian lessons from Bosnia … 170
8. Syria: the land of broken promises … 172
9. Assad is the problem, not the solution … 176

Libya. Reflections from October to May 2013 … 181
1. *Zenga Zenga* Democracy … 182
2. The untold story of Libya's Mahmud Gebril … 184

Turkey. Reflections from September 2011 to June 2013 … 191
1. Have we lost Turkey? … 193
2. What would you do if you were Erdoğan? … 195
3. Is Taksim the Turkish Tahrir? I thought not, until I came to Istanbul … 197
4. Judy asks: is Turkey becoming more Western or less? … 200

Jordan. Some reflections … 205
1. And revolution again in Jordan … 207

Lebanon. Some reflections … 213

Further reflections on the European disaster in the Arab World **219**
  1. EU-Egypt Task Force: the perfect misunderstanding   220
  2. How the EU is losing its entire Neighbourhood   222

Bibliography   225

I
FOREWORD
By Guy Verhofstadt

A Mediterranean Community
A New Vision for the European Southern Neighbourhood

A changed world since 2009

On 4 June 2009, US president Barack Obama gave a historic speech at Cairo University. The title of the speech was "A New Beginning". No-one could have predicted how radical that new beginning would be. Just 18 months later, on 14 January 2011, president Zine Al Abidine Ben Ali fled Tunisia after a month of protest, following the self-immolation of Mohamed Bouazizi, a fruit and vegetable seller in Tunisia. The entire world was surprised. It was the start of a series of events that changed the world.

What first looked like an 'Arab spring' transformed month by month into an Arab revolution. Protests started up in Yemen, Egypt, Libya, Bahrain, Morocco, Jordan, Syria and even Saudi Arabia. Dictators fell in Egypt, Libya and Yemen. For the first time since Kosovo in 1999, NATO intervened with a targeted aerial bombardment, this time in Libya. Protests in Syria against the regime of Bashar Al-Assad turned into a devastating war that has torn the country apart, causing more than 140,000 deaths, displacing half the country's population and destabilising the entire neighbourhood, as a result involving not only the main players of the Middle East, but also the global superpowers.

Protests did not hit only the Arab world. Citizens contested governments massively in Brazil, Turkey, Thailand, Sudan, Mexico, Malaysia, Ukraine, Venezuela and even the United States, where Occupy Wall Street rallied against the (lack of) morality of the financial markets. It looked like the world was seeing a new 1968, or even an 1848, when protesters no longer accepted the political order in which they were living.

Many of the eruptions find their roots in the financial and economic crisis that hit the world in 2008, the consequences of which are still being felt worldwide. Not only did the crisis suddenly make many people a lot poorer, it also changed the geopolitical paradigm. The two most important victims, politically speaking, were the United States and Europe. The crisis demanded that both powers invested a lot of time, energy and money into domestic affairs in order to put their affairs in order again. In both Unions it also changed public opinion, which became increasingly inward looking. Both lost power and influence on the world stage.

One example of this changing world order took place at the Climate Summit in Copenhagen in 2009. When the summit was about to finish without conclusion, President Obama asked for a meeting with India's Prime Minister Manmohan Singh. He received the answer that Singh had already left for India. Suspicious, Obama went to Singh's suite, where he found the latter sitting around the table with leaders from China, Russia, Brazil and South Africa. These 'new powers' were making a deal without the 'old powers', the United States and Europe.

The (re-)emergence of the 'new powers' also became clear in the war of Syria. The United States was on the brink of attacking Syria in August 2013, but had to back off when Russia entered the game. Today it is clear that there will be no solution in Syria without the agreement of Russia or Iran. On 1 January 2010, Russia started a Customs Union with Belarus and Kazakhstan. The Union is likely to be enlarged with Kirgizstan, Tajikistan, Turkmenistan and even Armenia and almost Ukraine, were it not of a second revolution.

Probably the most important change in world politics at the moment is the retreat of the United States from the Middle East. There are several reasons for this retreat. First of all, the US knows that it can't play ball in all parts of the world. Some choices have to be made. Secondly, the wars in Iraq and Afghanistan absorbed an enormous budget, with too many soldiers coming home in body bags and little prospect of real progress in either country. Thirdly, as the US is betting more and more on energy independence by drilling for new oil and searching for shale gas, the oil and gas providing countries of the Middle East have become less important. Fourth, no matter what the United States tries to do in the Arab world, it always seems to lose friends and appeal. Fifth, even though Israel is still seen as one of America's most important partners, the Israeli cause seems less and less attractive. The fact that Israeli Prime Minister Netanyahu publicly supported Mitt Romney in the presidential elections hasn't helped the Israeli cause either. No wonder that Samantha Power, America's ambassador to the UN and strategic advisor to the president, proposed that Obama make a shift in US foreign policy towards Asia, and away from the Arab world.

Finally, it is clear that the United States is becoming less and less interested in the European Union. They find the EU too complex, too slow and too unpredictable. Another long time grievance is the lack of military spending by the EU. Why should the US further invest in NATO if the EU refuses to take on board its military responsibilities? In the case of Libya, the US refused to get involved in an intervention until the last minute. Then it decided to 'lead from behind'… Quite a change compared to the world before 2009.

A European in Cairo: rowing against the current

Though the United States has the option to retract resources from the Middle East, the European Union is in a completely different position. The Middle East is our backyard, and we are theirs. Trade and migration flows, cultural and economic exchange, all force themselves upon us. Nevertheless, from 2009 onwards, the EU acted as if it had the same options available to it as the United States. We became disrupted by the most important battle in the history of the Union: overcoming the economic and financial crisis that threatened the very foundations of the Union. We became so focused on our internal problems, that we stopped looking abroad.

The ALDE group (The Alliance of Liberals and Democrats for Europe) in the European Parliament decided to go against this current and to recognise the historical significance of the Arab Spring. We visited Cairo as the revolution was unfolding at Tahrir Square – the first parliamentary group to do so. We also invited Mahmud Jibril – then the new and unknown leader of the National Transitional Council – to Europe. He went on to become the most important voice of liberalism/secularism in North Africa.

What started off as a sequence of loose initiatives, crystalized into a structural commitment of the ALDE group to the Arab Revolution when we decided to send a representative to Cairo on a long-term mission. The task fell on my chief of staff and the author of this book, Koert Debeuf. He had sufficient political experience and, more importantly, a passion for the Arab world and a thorough knowledge of its rich history. In the three years he was there, he delivered on the three major objectives for which he had been sent.

First of all, he gave us insight into a region we did not understand very well. What had really happened in our Southern Neighbourhood and what would come next? Several gaps were filled with reports, debates and constant feedback on the most recent evolutions in the Arab world. He wrote numerous articles and blogs stimulating debate in the ALDE group, in the European Parliament and in a much wider European and Arab sphere. Because of our permanent representative in Cairo, the ALDE group is able to act on current and accurate information. Koert, for example, was the first political official to enter Syria and report on the dramatic humanitarian crisis. This was a catalyst in the EU changing its strategy on aid in northern Syria.

Secondly, because of the efforts of the ALDE group's permanent representative in Cairo, we are proud to say we are able to support various political parties in North Africa and the Middle East. This is something Western Europe failed to do after the fall of the Berlin Wall, with a lot of political and economic instability as the consequence. We train politicians and their parties in Egypt and Tunisia and work with the National Forces Alliance in Libya, the only country where a liberal party won post-revolution elections.

Thirdly, thanks to our presence in the Arab world, we can create networks between political leaders and activists. Koert established contacts between them and gave activists a voice in Europe. He brought many Arab leaders and activists to the European Parliament: Amr Moussa (Egypt), Mahmud Gebril (Libya), Néguib Chebbi and Yassine Brahim (Tunisia), Ahmad Hariri (Lebanon), Fawaz Tello (Syrian opposition), Rami Jarah, Deiaa Dughmoch, Dany Abdul Dayem (Syrian activists) and Salim Idriss (General Commander of the FSA). For most, their visit to the ALDE group was their first appearance on the world stage. It gave them a platform and meant their voices could be heard globally.

In September 2012, Arab Leaders for Freedom and Democracy was established. A network unique in its kind, it enables top Arab leaders to inform each other of crucial events and help each other out.

Wins and losses in the EU's foreign policy

Although the ALDE group is perhaps unique in its strong involvement in the Arab world, one must admit that, during the past five years, the EU's foreign policy has made a transformation. Not only has the European External Action Service been built up, it has also done serious work. The most important 'win' was – without doubt – the landmark agreement on 13 April 2013 between Serbia's Prime Minister Ivica Dačić and Kosovo's Prime Minister Hashim Thaçi to begin reconciliation efforts. As a consequence, Serbia started EU membership talks on 21 January 2014.

A second 'win' was the deal struck with Iran on 25 November 2013. Although the EU was only one of the negotiators of the so-called P5+1 (the five permanent members of the UN Security Council plus Germany), the EU's High Representative, Catherine Ashton is generally credited with having kept the negotiations on the right track. In this deal, Iran agreed to scale down its enrichment of uranium and, in doing so, limit its nuclear activity to energy. In return, the EU eased some of its sanctions on 20 January 2014.

A third 'win' was the fact that Ashton was the only non-Egyptian allowed to visit deposed Egyptian president Mohamed Morsi where he was being hidden. The Egyptian government and the Muslim Brotherhood also allowed her and special envoy Bernardino Leon to try mediate between the two camps. When Morsi was still president of Egypt, a similar mediating effort was led between the presidency and the opposition. Although neither mediation brought results, the fact that both sides gave the EU a chance to try, indicates that European diplomacy has gained respect.

Nevertheless, as well as 'wins', there were a number of 'losses'. The most recent was Ukraine: days before Ukraine was due to sign an Association Agreement with the EU, it decided to cancel the deal and join the Russian Customs Union instead. It needed hundreds of thousands of people to protest against the deal with Russia and in favour of a European future, to turn this decision back. For the European Union, this came as a total surprise. Yet shouldn't the Commission have been alerted a few months earlier, when Armenia acted in this way? It is possible even that Georgia, Moldova and Azerbaijan will follow the same path. If they do, the entire Eastern Neighbourhood will have turned its back on the European Union and its policy.

From 1998 until 2006, most countries of the Southern Neighbourhood – Tunisia, Morocco, Algeria, Egypt, Jordan, Israel and Lebanon – signed a Euro-Mediterranean Agreement Establishing an Association. The Palestinian Authorities have an Interim Agreement, while Syria has initialled a Cooperation Agreement. Libya has no agreement at all, while Turkey is still (painfully) negotiating its membership.

Apart from Lebanon, Israel, the Palestinian Authorities and of course Turkey, all countries within this Euro-Mediterranean Agreement had dictatorships. Not one shared the basic values of the European Union: democracy and respect for human rights. A report of the European Court of Auditors on Egypt in 2013 also stated that there was almost no control over what happened to the European money – more specifically the budget support – given to the country. A report on the other countries would most probably give similar results. Although the basic conditions of this aid – more democracy and greater respect for human rights – were never met, the EU didn't change any of its agreements. However, this might have been understandable given the lack of perspective of change in the Arab region.

But when change did happen, the EU wasn't sufficiently supportive, not until the very last moment. Whereas Tunisia came as a surprise, Egypt could not be ignored. Instead of backing the demands of the people on Tahrir Square, the EU kept repeating messages that "all parties involved should refrain from violence". It wasn't until the very last evening before Mubarak was ousted that the EU asked him to listen to the people and step down. Even worse was the EU position on Bahrain: a top diplomat said that he understood the crackdown on the protesters taking to the streets and demanding their rights. So, it should not surprise us that the people of Tunisia, Egypt, Bahrain, Yemen, Morocco and Jordan felt left on their own by the EU, whilst risking their lives for European values. Nor should we be surprised when we are accused of having double standards.

The scenario in Libya and Syria, however, was different. In Libya, NATO (and thus the EU) intervened militarily and saved hundreds of thousands of lives. To be fair, it wasn't the EU but France and the UK who assumed the lead. And although the EU was the first to introduce sanctions on the Assad regime by blocking the bank accounts of its supporters and banning them from travelling, the people of Syria felt deserted when they needed humanitarian and logistic support, for it rarely reached those who needed it most.

The EU could have made up for its hesitation during the uprisings once the dictators were ousted. It could have come up with a plan, a vision supported by new funding in order to help the transition towards democracy. Egypt might have been reticent, but Libya, Tunisia and Jordan asked for more help. Instead, the EU did nothing more than repackage its old agreements, adding a few hundred million euro.

The result of the European absence is that other regional powers stepped in. Qatar started supporting the Muslim Brotherhood network in the entire region, from Morocco to Syria. When the Muslim Brothers took power in Egypt, Qatar provided loans. When the Muslim Brothers in Libya lost the elections, Qatar sponsored the opposition and some militias to make life difficult for the new government. When the Muslim Brotherhood was kicked out of power in Egypt, three other wealthy countries stepped in: Saudi Arabia, Kuwait and the United Arab Emirates.

While European money is considered difficult to obtain, Gulf money is easy. They don't ask for human rights or democracy, but for loyalty. Given the negotiations of the West with Iran, the Gulf is, more than ever, looking for allies. Turkey is playing its regional role as well. Since Ahmet Davutoglu's appointment as minister of foreign affairs, Turkey is looking more to the East than to the West. With a kind of neo-Ottoman agenda, Turkey is playing the card of being a model of democracy with a moderate (slow) Islamic agenda. In short, the Arab world seems to have become divided into two (Sunni) camps: Turkey and Qatar on the one hand; Saudi Arabia, Kuwait and the UAE on the other. In the meantime, Iran has been playing its own game, supporting Assad, Hezbollah, Hamas and Al Bashir's regime in Sudan.

Migration and the problems Europe is facing on the Italian islands and in the south of Spain and Greece might have been reason enough to engage more with the Southern Neighbourhood. We didn't do this due to the financial and economic crisis and thus a lack of will to invest in this region. But we must also admit we displayed a lack of vision. Even though Europe is still an attractive idea to many Arabs, there has been very little effort at rapprochement.

In summary, we can say that European foreign policy has gained visibility, respect and some important successes, but at the same time we are on the brink of losing our entire neighbourhood to powers like Russia, Qatar and Saudi Arabia, whose aims do not involve the promotion of democracy and human rights.

A vision for the Neighbourhood

Europe's neighbourhood has seen arguably the most intense changes of anywhere in the world in the past ten years. In November 2003, the people of Georgia ousted Soviet dinosaur Eduard Shevardnadze. One year later, the Ukrainians made president Viktor Yanukovych resign after rigged elections. Six years later it was the turn of Tunisia, Egypt and Libya to end decades-old dictatorships. The Kings of Morocco and Jordan were also pushed to reform.

The transformation of the entire European neighbourhood has only just begun. What we see today is only one of the stages of the transition to democracy. The people in both the Eastern and the Southern Neighbourhood have been fighting for their freedom and will never agree to a return to dictatorship. But the challenges are enormous. Each of the ousted regimes has left behind a country with a ruined economy and a wounded society. To rebuild these countries will take a lot of time, effort and money.

The power and the success of the European project has always been its conversion of poor dictatorships into prosperous democracies. That was the case for the founding member states, but also for countries like Greece, Spain, Portugal and all of the former European members of the Warsaw Pact. The European idea is spreading peace, democracy and wealth by uniting forces and welcoming all European countries to participate.

The United States immediately understood that a democratic, peaceful and prosperous Europe would be to its benefit. This would make of Europe a strategic partner and a substantial market. It would also prevent another devastating war that would threaten the United States as well. That was the reasoning behind the Marshall Plan and behind NATO: an alliance of democracies against non-democratic enemies. Seventy years later, no-one doubts this was the right strategy.

Today we are facing a similar situation: the European Union is witnessing a neighbourhood trying to rid itself of dictatorship. It is Europe's turn to take responsibility and support its neighbourhood to become peaceful, democratic and prosperous. It should make partners and markets of these countries, which is to the benefit of all. We cannot copy the ideas of the 1940s and recycle the Marshall Plan, NATO and European integration, but we cannot sit on our hands either and just let events take their course.

In documents of the European Commission on the Southern Neighbourhood you find the following programmes and instruments: Civil Society Facility; Venice Commission; European Endowment for Democracy; European Instrument for Democracy and Human Rights; European Neighbourhood and Partnership Instrument; Union for the Mediterranean; Security Sector Reform; EUBAM (EU Border Assistance Mission); EUPOL COPPS (EU Co-ordinating Office for Palestinian Police Support); Investment Security in the Mediterranean; Euro-Mediterranean Logistic Network LOGISMED; Association Action Plan; Deep and Comprehensive Free Trade Area; Instrument for Stability; Facility for Euro-Mediterranean Investment and Partnership; Neighbourhood Investment Facility; Macro Financial Assistance; Agreement on Conformity Assessment Acceptance of industrial products; Mobility Partnership; Mediterranean Science, Policy, Research and Innovation Gateway; Erasmus Mundus; Tempus and Euro-Med Youth Programme.

It is obvious that a combination of all these programmes is not the most inspiring way to convince people from both sides of the Mediterranean to cooperate more. The reality is that few citizens or even journalists in the Southern Neighbourhood have the slightest idea that the EU is running programmes on many levels in their country. Moreover, the sad reality is that the programmes are barely working. As the report of the Court of Auditors on Egypt clearly showed, the conditions of more democracy and respect for human rights are not met, while the EU has no idea how its budget support was spent. Even under the new principle of "more for more", nothing has really changed, as this policy is not combined with a "less for less" principle.

How can we expect people to be in favour of Europe and its values if they remain unaware of European efforts? Worse still, those who are favourable to these values feel left out in the cold by the EU. If we want to support those people fighting for democracy and human rights, we have to use more creativity and imagination rather than merely relying on the current spider web of agreements and programmes originally signed with dictators and executed by malfunctioning bureaucracies.

A Mediterranean Community

The problem of the current Association Agreements is that it gives the neighbouring countries a sense of satisfaction of having signed an agreement with the European Union, but has little to do with partnership and almost nothing with ownership. The typical North-South philosophy is one of the reasons why these neighbouring countries don't feel particularly comfortable with the association frameworks. They merely see it as a way of receiving money. And if they can get a better deal elsewhere, they will jump to the other sponsor without much regret.

Therefore it is necessary to turn this North-South divide around. To ensure ownership we have to create a community rather than an association. Both the EU and its neighbouring countries must be considered equally responsible 'owners' of the community. Given the differences between the Eastern and the Southern Neighbourhood, we will here focus on the South and propose the creation of a Mediterranean Community.

The Mediterranean Community would be a community between the EU and its member states and the following countries: Morocco, Algeria, Tunisia, Libya, Egypt, Jordan, Israel, the Palestinian Authorities,

Lebanon and Syria. Obviously every one of these countries needs to fulfil democratic and economic conditions.

The idea behind this Mediterranean Community is to streamline all possible programmes the EU can offer: trade, education, visa requirements, energy, migration, border control... To be clear, we are not talking about a simple repackaging of current agreements, but about bringing each programme to a higher level. A key area to address is education, one of the biggest problems in the Arab world. We must give more young people the opportunity to study in Europe. In 2013, only 159 students from the Southern Neighbourhood were allowed to study a year in Europe through the Erasmus Mundus programme. It should be much more. At the same time, we should bring more teachers and students to the Southern Mediterranean and invest in education there. This is the most efficient way of helping these countries to move forward.

The success of the European project has always been that countries who become members are more successful than those who don't. That's why only very few (rich) countries decided not to join the project. It seems that we are more or less reaching the boundaries of the EU enlargement. After the Western Balkans, there is little public support to go further. However, it would be a mistake to think that the European project is fully realized. With this mindset, things can only decline.

The power and attraction of the European Union is its legacy as the most efficient tool of peace, democracy and prosperity in history. The investment of time, energy and money into this project, and into those countries joining the project, has proven to be the best investment ever made – just as the Marshall Plan and NATO are the best investment the United States has ever made. As the US is now retreating from the European neighbourhood, it is up to the EU to step in and use a method that has proven itself: creating communities. Europe has to create the dream it has represented for so long to so many citizens. That is why we have to build this new Mediterranean Community.

As Tunisia is clearly making more progress than the other Southern Mediterranean countries, the EU can start its Mediterranean Community there. When the other countries see the benefits, and when their citizens see the opportunities, joining the new Mediterranean Community will quickly become an attractive idea. Citizens will realize it is better to live within the Mediterranean Community than outside of it. Just as Slovenia was a model for the other countries of former Yugoslavia by joining the European Union, Tunisia can become a model for the Arab world by joining the Mediterranean Community. In that case, it might only be a matter of years before Egyptian citizens wave the European flag on Tahrir Square, because it means more democracy, more security and more prosperity for them and for their children.

Guy Verhofstadt
President of the ALDE Group
Brussels, 3 February 2014

This Is an Arab Revolution

– *"C'est une révolte?"*
– *"Non, Sire, ce n'est pas une révolte, c'est une révolution."*
Duc de la Rochefoucauld-Liancourt to Louis XVI, 1789

On 1 September 2011, the day I arrived in Cairo with my family, I received a telephone call from the Egyptian embassy in Brussels. There was a problem with my presence in Egypt. My family and my former colleagues in the European Parliament were panicking. When a friend called his old friend, the Egyptian minister of international cooperation, he was shocked to hear she knew everything about me. She knew where my house was, where my children would be going to school and – of course – the exact day I had arrived. She told him that my activities were not welcome in Egypt. When my friend asked what I should do, the minister answered immediately: "He should pack his bags and leave the country".

As a 'welcome present' to the Arab spring that could count, I realized that, seven months after President Hosni Mubarak had been ousted (after eighteen days of protests on Tahrir Square), the revolution wasn't over. But that shouldn't have come as a surprise. After the fall of the Berlin Wall in 1989 and the collapse of the Soviet Union in 1991, the countries of Central Europe didn't become fully-fledged democracies overnight. I remember well that the people of Poland could choose between no fewer than ninety political parties in their first parliamentary elections. Everyone wanted to have his own party. There was even a Party of the Beer Drinkers. We also saw how people thought democracy would bring paradise at once. Disappointed in every president and government that came, the Polish people consequently sacked each of them in every follow-up election. It took more than twenty years before a prime minister (Donald Tusk) succeeded in being elected for a second term. We often forget how messy politics was, and still is, in many of the former communist countries, even though the European Union did everything it could to help and support them.

The fall of the Berlin Wall in 1989 came totally unexpected. Amid confusion and lack of clear orders, thousands of East Berlin citizens crossed the border on the evening of 9 November. On the very same evening, Berliners from West and East started to demolish this symbol of separation, injustice and dictatorship. The rest of the world was perplexed.

Sure, there were some signs – not least in Hungary, where people started to cut holes in the fence of the Iron Curtain in June 1989 – but few observers really saw the importance of it. However, when the Berlin Wall fell, people from all over Europe jumped in their cars and drove to Berlin to join the historic celebrations. I didn't. At sixteen, I was just old enough to realize that something big was happening, but unfortunately too young to drive to Berlin.

This first wave of revolutions took two years to change the world. Not only the Berlin Wall collapsed, it was also the end of communist dictatorships in Poland, Hungary, Czechoslovakia, Yugoslavia, Romania, Bulgaria, Lithuania, Latvia and Estonia and, in 1991, the Soviet Union itself. The West was euphoric. In these two years, the ideological war between communism and capitalism, between democracy and dictatorship, had come to an end – with a clear and decisive victor. The events inspired political scientist and economist Francis Fukuyama to write his *The End of History and the Last Man* (1992). From then on, we thought, we had only to wait until all the other countries of the world recognized the supremacy of liberal democracy, the rule of law and free markets.

My family had a weak spot for Poland. During the martial law of 1981, my uncle had smuggled food and clothes from Belgium into Poland in the middle of winter. There he met with the leaders of Solidarność, who were at that time hiding in the famous church of Chestochowa. One day, in 1982, one of the priests active in Solidarność stood at our front door. After he had told for more than an hour the most fascinating stories I ever heard, he gave me a sticker of Solidarność, which I proudly stuck on my toy box. I remember clearly the moment he said goodbye at our front door: we were staying in the comfort of our cosy home, while he was going back to resist dictatorship and fight for freedom.

In the 2000s, a second wave of revolutions seemed to prove Fukuyama right. It started in Belgrade, where a student movement, OTPOR, managed to coordinate the resistance against Slobodan Milošević. After a few months, they succeeded in getting rid of him. In 2003, the Rose Revolution led by Mikail Saakashvili ousted Soviet dinosaur Eduard Shevardnadze. In 2004, people filled Independence Square in Kiev to protest rigged presidential elections that had brought Victor Yanukovich to power. It was an exhilarating time. Again, I wished I could be there, but at the time I was working as an advisor to the prime minister of Belgium. Thanks to this position I was able to meet with people like Saakashvili and Yulia Timoshenko (Victor Yushchenko's co-revolutionary), but, of course, this was not the same as *being there*, on the square, sharing the hopes and the fears of the people.

On the evening of 14 January 2011, I was in Amsterdam, where I had a meeting with Farid Tabarki, a Dutch friend of Tunisian origin. He was constantly distracted by telephone calls from his father. When I asked what was going on, he replied that Tunisian president Ben Ali might be resigning in the hours to come. I was shocked. Why hadn't I seen this coming? Of course we had all heard on the news about violent protests in a few Tunisian cities – but who would have thought this would result in a dictator fleeing his country? While on the train back to Brussels, Farid called to say: "Ben Ali is gone." Due to a lengthy train delay, I had plenty of time to reflect. The film of 1989 played through my mind, I wasn't sixteen anymore... I could jump into that car and go to Tunis! I just had to decide when.

But events were quicker than I. After Tunisia came Egypt. Then Yemen. Then Libya and Bahrain. Protests started in Morocco, Jordan and Syria. We saw an 'Arab 1989' unfolding. It makes sense to call it a third wave of revolutions. The dictatorships in the Arab world were established in the slipstream of the post World War II socialist dream. Gamal Abdel Nasser removed the Egyptian King in 1952 and then installed a military-socialist regime. In Libya, Muammar Gaddafi followed suit in 1969. In Syria, Hafez Al Assad (the father of current Syrian president Bashar Al-Assad) came to power in 1970. Each of them – as well as Sadam Houssein in Iraq – was inspired by the Ba'ath party, a socialist pan-Arab political party that was first established in Syria in 1943.

Their ties with the Soviet Union were obvious to all. When Nasser kicked out the French and the British during the Suez Crisis of 1956, it was the Russians who paid for and built the Aswan Dam. During my stays in Syria with the Free Syrian Army, I was surprised to see that the majority of the Syrian generals spoke fluent Russian. They had all been trained in Russia, or in one of its former satellite states. Even when a country like Egypt turned away from the Soviet Union and chose an alliance with the United States, the Soviet-like intelligence apparatus remained in place. This is true even today – as I discovered that first day I arrived in Cairo, when I learned that the government knew everything about me and my family.

Atlantic centrism

When I first visited the Middle East in 2009, on a holiday in Lebanon, I was shocked by my lack of knowledge. As a historian, I of course knew about the Phoenicians and their inventing the alphabet. I knew about the Egyptian pharaohs and the legacy of Alexander the Great in the city of Alexandria. And we, Europeans, are proud of the defeat of the mighty Persians by the tiny Greek city-states in 5th century BC. We all know that Carthage was defeated after the threat of Hannibal and his elephants. However, after the death of Cleopatra in 30 BC, our knowledge becomes blurred. Sure, in the 7th century Mohamed founded Islam, but more than that we do not tend to know.

The only time the Arab world, or the Islamic world, appears in our history books is when they have been a 'threat to our civilisation'. The Battle of Poitier in 732, in which the Frankish leader Charles Martel defeated the Islamic troops and 'saved Europe'. The Crusades, when our knights had to liberate Jerusalem from the intolerant Muslims and safeguard Christian access to Christian holy places. The fall of Constantinople in 1453, when we 'lost' the capital of the Byzantine Empire to the Ottomans. The same Ottomans even came all the way up to Vienna twice (in 1529 and 1683) but were 'luckily' defeated. These moments were the 9/11s of the Middle Ages. They left us with the impression that the Arab World and its Islamic troops had only one goal: to destroy our Western Judeo-Christian civilization.

Apart from these confrontations, Westerners generally have no idea what happened in the Arab world between the death of Cleopatra and the foundation of the State of Israel. We know that, in 1798, Napoleon invaded Egypt and found a 'backward society'. He brought in a team of scientists and historians to record what was left of this great Pharaonic society. It were the French who rediscovered the pyramids and the old temples, deciphered the hieroglyphs and composed an 'Egyptian encyclopaedia': the '*Description de l'Égypte*'. The other prominent image we tend to have of the Arab world is of Lawrence of Arabia, the British soldier who finally succeeded in uniting the quarrelling Arabian tribes. Yet, the moment they get the opportunity to govern liberated Damascus, they make a complete mess of it...

However, the Christian West did have a weak spot for the Arab world, in particular, for the world of *One Thousand and One Nights*, the Arabia of the harems, the Turkish bath, polygamy, the mystery behind the women's veil. It is the Arabia of sensuality and sexuality. Everything that was forbidden in the Christian morality appeared to be possible behind the thick Arabian walls. It is this combination of ignorance and romanticism that Edward Said called 'Orientalism'. In his famous book of the same name (1978), Said explores the incidence of Orientalism in a vast amount of Western literature and art on the Arab world. Certainly in the 19th century, the age of Romanticism, the Arab world was pictured as a refined but decadent – and thus forbidden – world.

That changed in the second half of the 20th century. With the foundation of Israel in 1948, the Arab world again came to mean 'trouble'. There were the wars with Israel in 1948, 1967 and 1973, the Suez Crisis, the oil crisis, the war between Iran and Iraq, the civil wars in Lebanon and in Algeria, the terrorist attacks by Algerians in France. The fact that more than a million Algerians were killed in their war of independence seems not to bother Westerners much. Instead, we watch the news of the hijacking and bombing of planes by the Palestinians of Yasser Arafat and the Libyans of Muammar Gaddafi, the frightening Islamic revolution of Ayatollah Khomeini and his declaration of war on the West, the first and the second intifada, the terrorist attacks on US embassies, Saddam Hussein's invasion of Kuwait, followed by the First Gulf War, the attacks by the PKK in Turkey, Hamas in Gaza, Hezbollah in Lebanon, Al Qaeda in Afghanistan.

But most of that was pretty far away... until 2001 and the Al Qaeda terrorist attack on American soil. This horrific event was followed by the Istanbul bombings, the train attack in Madrid, the metro attack in London and many other attacks worldwide. The whole world was on red alert. In 2006, my colleague, the Prime Minister's security advisor, told me to stay away from the centre of Brussels between Christmas and New Year. The city even cancelled its traditional fireworks on New Year's Eve. Osama Bin Laden, the face of evil, delivered Koranic verses about Allah and jihad. It brought us face to face with our historic fear of the Arab and Islamic world.

Where Orientalism had tempered our ignorance with a flavour of sympathetic sensuality for a few centuries, we were now back to the predominance of the Middle Ages, the old mixture of ignorance and existential fear. American president George Bush spoke even of a new Crusade and of the 'Axis of Evil'. There was the feeling that danger was just around the corner. In the back rooms of mosques in every country, young people were being recruited for jihad. After the terrorist attacks in

New York, London and Madrid, we believed that there must be sleeping terrorist cells waiting for the right moment to strike.

When you live for a while in the Arab world, you realize that our ignorance is distorting the way we look at the world. You start to realize Westerners have a feeling of cultural superiority. We all learned at school that civilisation basically started in Greece and then went on to Rome. After the fall of Rome in 476, we went through a dark period called the Middle Ages. But in the 15th century, we 'rediscovered the light'. We invented book printing, science and art. We discovered the Americas and the rest of the world. We used our Greek and Roman heritage to start the Renaissance, which led to the Enlightenment, the Industrial Revolution and finally to the point we are at now, and where we assume we always have been: on top of the world.

You don't have to read a lot to realize how wrong and Eurocentric this view is. We need just to do one exercise… I think we will all agree that New York was the most significant city of the 20th century. Though not the capital, New York was the most important city of the most powerful country. It was also the largest city in the world. In the 19th century, the most important city was London, no doubt. It was the capital of the British Empire, the largest empire ever. London was also the epicentre of the Industrial Revolution earlier that century. If we go back two thousand years, we can confidently say that Rome was the most important city in the world. It was the capital of the Roman Empire and the 'global' centre of politics, art and architecture. We know also that, when Jesus was born, Rome was the largest city in the world.

There is a clear correlation between the importance of a city and its number of inhabitants. In the case of New York, London and Rome, the largest city of the world was also the most important one. It was at that moment the political, economical and cultural capital of the world. But as sure as we are about New York, London and Rome, we are much less certain about the top cities in the centuries in between. What were the largest cities of the world between Rome and London? And what about the time before Rome? The following list by Ian Morris (*Why the West Rules – For Now*, 2010), gives an overview:

City	Year	Population
Uruk	3000 BCE	Over 45,000
Memphis	2000	60,000
Uruk, Thebes	1500	75,000
Babylon, Thebes	1200	80,000
Qi (China)	1000	25,000
Babylon	500	150,000
Alexandria	200	300,000
Rome	1 CE	1,000,000 (?)
Rome	400	800,000
Chang'an	600	250,000
Chang'an	800	1,000,000
Kaifeng	1000	1,000,000
Hangzhou	1200	800,000
Nanjing	1400	500,000
Beijing	1500	600,000
Beijing	1600	700,000
Beijing	1700	650,000
Beijing	1800	1,100,000
London	1900	6,600,000
New York	1950	12,500,000
Tokyo	2000	26,700,000

It is quite surprising to see that, apart from New York, London and Rome, not one 'Western' city has ever been the largest city in the world. Of course, one could argue it is not entirely fair to include China and the Far East in the list. There is some truth in that. Even though there was an exchange of ideas and products between both sides of the Indus River, there was no real interaction between these two entities. Furthermore, the agricultural revolution occurred on both sides of the river yet apart from each other. If we make a new list that concentrates on the largest cities of the world on the Western side of the Indus River, we get the following result:

City	Year	Population
Uruk	3000 BCE	Over 45,000
Memphis	2000	60,000
Uruk, Thebes	1500	75,000
Babylon, Thebes	1200	80,000
Susa	1000	25,000
Babylon	500	150,000
Alexandria	200	300,000
Rome	1 CE	1,000,000 (?)
Rome	400	800,000
Constantinople	600	500,000
Damascus	800	125,000
Cordoba	1000	200,000
Bagdad, Cairo, Constantinople	1200	250,000
Cairo	1400	125,000
Constantinople	1500	100,000
Constantinople (Istanbul)	1600	400,000
Constantinople, London	1700	600,000
London	1800	900,000
London	1900	6,600,000
New York	1950	12,500,000
New York	2000	16,700,000

This overview makes clear that, since the beginning of human civilisation, the capitals of the Western world were located mainly in the Middle East and North Africa. The birth of Islam didn't change that. On the contrary, during the first thousand years of Islamic civilisation, capitals like Damascus, Cordoba, Bagdad, Cairo and Constantinople (Istanbul) made European cities look like villages. The centre of the West only moved back to Europe, and later to the United States, during the Age of Revolution: the Glorious Revolution, the Industrial Revolution, the American Revolution and the French Revolution.

Is Cairo the next New York?

I visited Cairo in March 2011, one month after President Hosni Mubarak had been deposed. What struck me most was the energy hanging in the air. The entire city was electrified by the new feeling of freedom and empowerment. Every Egyptian I met was in a kind of a trance; Egypt had done what everyone else thought was impossible. In one of the conferences, the translator seemed to be reporting the final of the Football World Cup, except – of course – that Egypt had won.

You could *smell* history in the air of Cairo and there was this strange feeling of rhythm, the drums of change. I recognised this rhythm from my visit to Berlin three years after the fall of the Wall. Checkpoint Charlie was still there and the differences between East and West Berlin remained stark, but the city was breathing freedom – yes, even anarchy. People had defeated the system that had imposed this ludicrous separation and oppression on them. The newly gained freedom gave the city a boost of energy and creativity.

I felt a rhythm in London, in Beijing and in New York too, in crescendo. London is still the largest city of Europe and it is very much alive. It is the European capital of think tanks, of financial markets, of contemporary art. In and around London, you still find the best universities in the world. However, when compared to Beijing, London's rhythm is pretty slow. The Chinese are determined to climb the social ladder and are working day and night for it. Their children must be first in their class at school in order to receive a scholarship to the best schools. In Beijing, you find the most modern architecture as well as an exploding art scene. In Beijing, you can feel the rhythm so acutely that when you go back to Europe, you have to adjust to slowing down.

And then there is New York City! The first time I walked on Times Square at midnight, it didn't feel like the middle of the night at all: all shops were open, crowds crisscrossed all over the square, non-stop shows on Broadway, and on the corner of the square was the building of the *New York Times*, still the most important newspaper in the world. As I was travelling with the Belgian prime minister, I had the opportunity to attend a session of the General Assembly and the Security Council of the United Nations. Almost all presidents and prime ministers of the planet are gathering at the United Nations in New York trying to be heard. Many of them regret they don't have the time to visit the city's museums, some of the best in the world.

"If I can make it there, I can make it anywhere. It's up to you. New York, New York," sang Frank Sinatra in 1980. However, something has changed. The great writers, artists or entrepreneurs might still be living in London or New York, but there is increasingly less place for the upcoming ones. Prices for apartments or flats have become so high that you can only afford to live in these two cities if you have already made it in life. For those who still want to make it, living in London or New York is simply not an option anymore. While the average rent in 2013 in London was almost $2000, in New York it was already more than $3000. The Lou Reeds, Andy Warhols or Frederick Bastiats of today have to look for options other than New York. This real estate challenge is changing the very nature of the 'capital of the world'. The same happened to Paris. Café de Flor or Les Deux Magots are no longer the place for young thinkers and writers like Camus, Sartre or Hemingway to discuss their new ideas or to write their vanguard books. Paris has become a nostalgic place for the educated and affluent. And renting a place in Montmartre, where Picasso, Modigliani, Van Gogh and Apollinaire lived, is only possible if you have a top job. Young talent has been pushed out of the centre of Paris.

That other famous line of Sinatra's song – 'the city that never sleeps' – would today be 'a city that never sleeps'. A recent study by Marion Roberts looked into the volume of bank payments done by night, worldwide. New York is only 32nd on the list. A lot of Spanish cities are in the top ten, but the number one 'city that never sleeps' is Cairo. This may come as a surprise, but not if you have been there. In Cairo, people have dinner at 11 pm or even midnight. You can be stuck in a traffic jam at 2 am. Protests on Tahrir Square and fights with the police went on until around 5 am. Then there was quiet until 8 am. There is no standardised timeframe; some live in the morning, others live at night.

Cairo is also more or less the same size as New York. There are no reliable official figures, but everyone agrees the city has more than 20 million inhabitants. People literally live everywhere. Some 2 million live in the old graveyard of the city, where graves have the shape of little houses. It is fascinating to see how very alive the so-called 'Death City' is. Other people are living on the roofs of apartment buildings, or in the gardens of deserted houses.

It would be an exaggeration to conclude that Cairo is now the number one city of the world. But one cannot ignore the city's pace. While this beat is fading in Berlin, London or New York, it is clearly accelerating in Cairo. Some call it chaos, but it is more than just chaos. So much is happening that you have to follow the news day and night to stay up-to-date. Former President of Egypt, Mohamed Morsi, announced his cancellation of a new tax law at 3 am on Facebook. His minister of foreign affairs resigned at 2 am. Press conferences are held in the morning, but also at midnight. Important trials generally start at 9 or 10 am, but the 2012 presidential debate between Amr Moussa and Abdel Moneim Aboul Fotouh started at 9 pm and ended at 2 am.

These crazy hours can be explained partly by climate, lack of organisation or inefficiency. But that does not reveal the full picture. In Cairo, and in the entire Arab world of today, there is not enough time in a normal day to absorb everything that is happening. Where in Europe or the United States there are perhaps a couple of major news stories a week, in the Arab world (indeed just in Egypt) there are one or two stories every day – sometimes more. In trying to follow and understand what is happening, one is always short on eyes and ears. Whenever I return from Europe or the US to the Arab world, I have to put myself into a higher gear to be able to keep up.

More than an Arab Spring

The term 'Arab Spring' was first used in 2005. In January that year, the first democratic elections were held in Iraq. These historic elections were seen as a victory for the democracy promotion agenda of US president George Bush. On 14 February, Rafiq Hariri, the long serving prime minister of Lebanon, was assassinated in a car bomb in Beirut. As it was immediately clear that Syria was behind this assassination, huge protests took the streets of Beirut, demanding real democracy and that Syria get out of the country. This was the birth of the 14 March movement, lead by Rafiq's son, Saad Hariri. Also in 2005, Egypt had its first 'open' presidential elections; for the first time, Hosni Mubarak stood against contenders. One of the opposition leaders, Ayman Nour, decided to run for president.

Conservative American commentators wondered if these events were signs of an "Arab Spring". The term referred to the Prague Spring, the short-lived liberalization and democratization process in Czechoslovakia in 1968, under the leadership of Alexander Dubcek, before it was crushed by Soviet tanks. It is clear that using the term 'spring' was pretty cynical. And cynical it was meant to be. Nobody believed that a real democratization process was possible in the Middle East. Dictators like Hosni Mubarak would not let this happen. And indeed, he didn't. Ayman Nour was jailed during the presidential campaign and stripped of all his political rights. Under pressure from the European Parliament and the US administration, he was freed, but then locked up again for many years.

The term 'Arab Spring' reappeared on 6 January 2011 in a piece by Colum Lynch in *Foreign Policy*. At this stage, Tunisian dictator Ben Ali hadn't fled the country yet and we were twenty days away from the protests on Egypt's Tahrir Square. Tunisians were, however, asking the regime to leave and there had been some clashes in other countries, leading Lynch to raise the question: were these signs of Obama's Arab Spring? On 14 January, the day Ben Ali was ousted, the editorial of American newspaper *Christian Science Monitor* was entitled 'Arab Spring? Or Arab Winter?' On 25 January, in an interview in German magazine *Der Spiegel,* Mohamed El Baradei was quoted as saying: "Perhaps we are currently experiencing the first signs of an 'Arab Spring'".

Though the term 'Arab Spring' has persisted, the reference to the Prague Spring soon disappeared. It was clear that what was happening in the Arab world was a lot bigger than the short upwelling of liberty in the former Republic of Czechoslovakia. After the ousting of Ben Ali in Tunisia, Mubarak in Egypt, Saleh in Yemen and Gaddafi in Libya, analysts and politicians looked for another frame of reference. Soon, comparisons with the fall of the Berlin Wall and the collapse of the Soviet Union appeared in talks between Western leaders and in newspapers, magazines and academic journals. After all, the philosophy of the Baath parties in Iraq and Syria and the pan-Arab ideas of former Egyptian president Nasser were socialist. And many Arab politicians had firm links with Moscow and the Communist party.

But soon that comparison was dismissed for being too optimistic as well. The two key grounds for this scepticism were the lack of democratic history in the Arab world and, of course, Islam. Many analysts wrote that communism and the Warsaw Pact were just a brief mistake. The Eastern European countries had always been an integral part of the European democratic history, they wrote. This interruption of fifty years was too short to change that. People were also educated enough to step over this gap easily and get back on the European track, where they belonged. Most analyses pointed out that the Arab world is a whole different ball game. No democratic history (which is not true), no history of secularism (also not true) and no educated masses able to carry the burden of democratic responsibility. In other words, the Arab Spring 'can't succeed because it is Arab'.

However, what finally buried the comparison with 1989 for most people was the Islam factor. Very few believe that democracy and Islam can go together. Islam, they say, is the religion of the sword and the Sharia. While Christianity converted and convinced people and countries of itself, Islam conquered and forced. Many don't only believe this is a fact of history, but also a fact of today. Look at Iran, Saudi Arabia, Afghanistan and Pakistan, where Taliban-ish governments cut off the hands of thieves and unjustly stone women? I will explain in the following chapters why this argument is not only prejudiced or even racist but also nonsense, historically inaccurate. After all, Indonesia with its 240 million inhabitants is the largest Muslim country and the third largest democracy in the world.

A tsunami of change

There are many signs that what we are currently witnessing in the Arab world is just the beginning. The Arab Spring is an earthquake, deep under the water. The toppling of dictators in 2011 has made some minor waves, but below the surface a massive wave is building. It is not clear when this tsunami of change will reach the surface, but when it does, it will be huge. It will affect every fibre of society.

There are many indicators of imminent large-scale change, but the main one is demographics. In the Arab world, half of the population is younger than 25. They are growing up in a society that is blocking their aspirations and ambitions. They feel that both the state and the organizational structures of their lives have been unfair to them: the lack of social mobility, the lack of freedom in marriage, the lack of freedom of speech, the desperate position of women, the unacceptable degree of poverty of the masses, the corruption, the backwardness of some interpretations of Islam. The entire fabric of society is a cage and it cannot hold the pressure of this young generation. They have access to information via the Internet. They read other opinions via Facebook, Twitter and blogs.

If you take a historical bird's eye view – zoom out from what is happening from day to day – you see that this is not just an Arab Spring. It's not even a third wave of democratic revolutions since 1989. It is much bigger than that. It is an Arab Revolution, with a capital R. It is a Revolution because it crystallises revolutions on several different levels. What we are facing are revolutions in communication, economy, social issues, religion, hierarchy and democratic organisation. There have been many books written about this huge new change: *Third Industrial Revolution* (Jeremy Rifkin, 2011), *The Third Wave* (Alvin Toffler, 1980), *The Network Society* (Manuel Castells, 2006), to mention just a few.

Historical comparisons always have shortcomings. "No man ever steps in the same river twice, for it's not the same river and he's not the same man," said the Greek philosopher Heraclitus. It is nevertheless important to look back in history in order to learn from it. That's why I will try to analyze that mother of all political revolutions: the French Revolution. Even though times are certainly different, there are more similarities than we think between it and the Arab Revolution.

The Arab versus the French Revolution

For many people, comparing the Arab Spring with the French Revolution is akin to blasphemy. It's like comparing one of our contemporary politicians to giants like Winston Churchill or Abraham Lincoln. Critics would argue that the French Revolution was about high ideals, the Enlightenment and the Declaration of the Rights of Man and of the Citizen, while none of this has been the case so far in the Arab world. On the contrary, Islamic fundamentalists and extremists have been replacing secular dictators. However, this point of view is not only short-sighted, it is usually based on a racist reading of history.

The causes of the French Revolution

The French Revolution had economical, social and political causes. It is commonly known that France was facing bankruptcy at the end of the 1780s. The country had a mountain of debt after it lost the Seven Years' War against Britain (1756–1763) and after the support it gave to the American War of Independence (1775–1783). Fighting to expand and defend its colonial power in order to be able to compete with Britain, France had invested a lot in its naval forces. The loans, and particularly the high interest rates it faced, led to a major financial crisis. On top of that, after a free trade agreement in cotton with Britain in 1786, most French cotton factories collapsed and unemployment and poverty spread all over the north of France.

At the same time, the French people carried a heavy tax burden. Citizens, certainly the peasants, were having difficulties feeding their families while the King and nobility were leading sumptuous lives. It made them hate the ruling classes. In the meantime, failed crops and harsh winters led to an increase in the price of bread, and starvation.

King Louis XVI tried to carry out reforms, appointing new ministers but quickly sacking them when the French nobility refused the proposed reforms. Galvanised by the ideas of the Enlightenment, more and more people started to call for reforms and for greater budget transparency. It was this struggle and blockade of the political system that made Louis XVI convene the Estates General for the first time since 1614.

The social ground for the French revolution had its roots in an unseen growth of population. In 1700, France had 20 million inhabitants; in 1789, the population had grown to 30 million. Paris had around 600,000 inhabitants, which made it the largest city in the world after London. A rapid growth of population always means a sharp rise of young, ambitious people. If there is no opportunity for social mobility, that ambition turns into frustration. In pre-revolutionary France, the guilds that regulated almost the entire economy kept their doors closed and limited the career opportunities for many others. In government, all offices were bought or inherited from father to son.

The political cause of the French Revolution was a combination of corruption, tyranny, the inability to reform, and the repressive police state. In most of his pamphlets. Voltaire did not attack the tyranny but the corruption of the bought offices, while Mirabeau attacked the lack of tax and budget reforms. The reign of terror was not purely political but also economic. As France forbade the import of popular Asian cotton, American tobacco and other products, people started to smuggle these into the country as a way to earn a supplementary income for their family. The anti-smuggling police, known as The Farm, started a war against these well-organized smugglers, which lead to many killings.

The causes of the Arab Revolution

The slogans used all over the Arab world during the uprisings were "We want the end of the regime" and "Freedom, dignity, social justice and bread". This summarized list of demands shows that the causes of the Arab Revolution too are economic, social and political. It is no accident that the Arab Revolution started with a street vendor, Mohamed Bouazizi.

The situation that led to his self-immolation shows us exactly what made the Arab world explode. He was a poor young man, no doubt dreaming about a better future, but stuck in a situation where survival was the only goal. While the in-laws of President Ben Ali, the Trabelsi family, lived a decadent life, Bouazizi had only one possession: the cart with which he transported his vegetables to sell on the street. In order to have this cart and these vegetables, he had had to mortgage all his family's possessions. When a police officer decided that he was not permitted to stand where he was on the street, she confiscated all his belongings. Just like that. No discussion.

The economic causes of the Arab revolution are obvious. Even though the economic situation in every country is different, there are economic problems everywhere. Twenty five percent of the Egyptians live below the poverty line. Thirty percent are not able to read or write. Bread and gas are heavily subsidized in order to enable the poor to survive. In none of the dictatorships it is possible to do business without paying off the ruling families. And when the younger generation (Bashar Al Assad, Ben Ali, Gamal Mubarak, Saif Al Islam Gaddafi) pretended to reform, they appeared only more corrupt than their (political) fathers.

This huge corruption, combined with a Kafkaesque bureaucracy, pushes a large amount of people into the informal (labour) market and unofficial housing. They live in permanent uncertainty as the police can close down their shops at any given moment. The police can confiscate their goods and take them to the police station, where many don't survive the treatment they receive. The corruption leads to a lack of proper investment in infrastructure, education and health and sends the economy into an almost unstoppable downwards spiral. The worldwide economic and financial crisis also hit – and continues to affect – the Arab world and has slowed down economic growth.

The social causes are perhaps even more powerful. The population of the Arab world exploded over the past few decades. During the past century, the populations of Egypt and Morocco multiplied more than fivefold. Egypt alone has 86 million inhabitants today. Cairo, with about 20 million inhabitants, is by far the largest city in Africa and the Middle East and one of the largest in the world. A majority of the people (50,3%) are younger than 25. Many positions, certainly in Egypt, are transferred from father to son. Unemployment for Arabs – again, certainly in Egypt – is disastrous. A man can only marry a woman if he has an apartment. No job means no apartment and thus no marriage. No marriage means that it is very hard, if not impossible, to have sexual intercourse. What cocktail can be more explosive?

The political causes of the Arab Revolution are a combination of corruption, dictatorship, unwillingness to reform and police brutality. While the Tunisians spontaneously hit the streets to protest against the regime, the Egyptian revolution was much better prepared. Protest organizations like Kefaya ("Enough") and the April 6 Youth Movement were already preparing to bring Gamal Mubarak down when the time came for him to succeed his father as president of Egypt. The Tunisian revolution speeded up everything. The famous Facebook page, "We are all Khaled Said"[1], was about police brutality. In Dera'a, Syria, people only took the streets after the security forces tortured a few kids after they had written "The people want the end of the regime" on an insignificant wall.

In short, it is clear that in both the French and the Arab revolution it was a combination of economic, social and political causes that rendered the people ready for revolution. In both revolutions, a majority of the people was struggling to survive while a corrupt upper class was taking an ever-larger part of the share. Both Louis XVI and the Arab dictators used terror and brutality to keep the people quiet. Both underestimated the social pressures that were to give an unexpected force to ideas of change.

A chronology of the French Revolution

On 5 May 1789, King Louis XVI summoned the convention of the Estates General in Versailles to discuss tax reform. The Third Estate didn't agree with the voting system by which the 25 million people they represented had the same weight as the other two, much smaller, Estates of Catholic clergy and nobility. The Third Estate moved to meet alone and first declared itself the National Assembly and then, on 9 July 1789, the National Constituent Assembly. It was the National Assembly that put in place the Declaration of Rights of Man and of the Citizen and abolished all bought and inherited offices in government.

As the revolutionary atmosphere increased and people continued gathering and protesting, soldiers started to pour into the streets of Paris.

---

[1] Khaled Said was a 28 Egyptian Internet activist who was killed in Alexandria by the police on 6 June 2010. His brother took a picture of his deformed face and put it online. It created uproar. Wael Gonim created the Facebook page "We are all Khaled Said", which immediately became a platform for Egyptians to express their anger with the brutality of the Mubarak regime.

On 14 July, a group of 954 people decided to take over the Bastille, an old prison in the centre of Paris and a hated symbol of tyranny. With only seven prisoners, the Bastille was as good as empty. What is not often mentioned is that the Revolution didn't start on a popular level with the storming of the Bastille, but with the sacking of the customs gates that encircled the city of Paris. From 11 to 14 July, professional and part-time smugglers joined merchants, petty traders, artisans, labourers and the unemployed in destroying no less than forty customs posts. Sacking the city, they broke and burned everything they could get their hands on.

As this is not the place to go over every detail of the events of the French revolution, I will turn to Crane Brinton's *The Anatomy of Revolution* (1965). In his study of the Glorious (English), the American, the French and the Russian revolutions, he finds a pattern of four phases:

1. THE RULE OF THE MODERATES

After the revolutionary events – in which people take the establishment by surprise and have to deal with a violent response in return – there is the catalyst that brings victory, followed by a brief 'honeymoon' period. This short period is followed by 'the rule of the moderates'. In France, this period was that of a Constitutional Monarchy. Although Louis XVI had to move from Versailles to the Tuileries in Paris, he stayed on as King of France. The major difference was that he had to allow a parliament to take decisions and write a constitution. In 1791, France had its first constitution. Leaders were the well-known 'Girondins' like Lafayette and Mirabeau. The main problem of the 'moderates' is that they do not succeed in delivering on the promises of the revolution. In the case of France, they also could not stop the violence as Austria and Prussia declared war and invaded France.

2. THE REIGN OF TERROR AND VIRTUE

At a certain point, French extremists started to take over power. Making use of the general turmoil in France, a well-organized group of radicals organized an attack on the Tuileries Palace in Paris and overthrew the monarchy on 10 August 1792. The Jacobins of Robespierre took all political power on 2 June 1793, when they arrested 22 'non-loyal' members of the National Convention, which replaced the National Assembly. The Convention, now in the hands of the extreme Jacobins, had executive powers and the task of drafting a new constitution. De facto, this power was exercised by the Convention's Committee of Public Safety to start their 'Reign of Terror'.

Under the leadership of 'The Incorruptable' Maximilien Robespierre, every 'corrupted' person – anyone against the revolution and its principles – risked death by guillotine. Alongside the Reign of Terror, there was also a 'Reign of Virtue'. The Jacobins used a religious rhetoric and organized meetings of the Supreme Being. They changed the names of streets and squares and put in place a new revolutionary calendar. They were against gambling, drunkenness, sexual irregularities of all sorts, and 'ostentatious displays' of poverty or idleness. Many of them took the liberty of enforcing abstention from these vices and insisted, with force, on the carrying out of positive acts of virtue. Meanwhile, a new Republican Constitution was approved by public referendum.

3. THERMIDOR

On 9 Thermidor of the Year II (27 July 1794), almost all members of the Convention conspired against Robespierre and deposed of him in the middle of a meeting. The day before, he had threatened (without naming anyone) all those involved in conspiracies against him. The next day, he was executed without trial together with 21 of his closest associates. The Thermidorian regime ended the Reign of Terror, granting people more freedom, especially in the area of religion, while royal sentiments were again tolerated. However, this regime started its own 'White Terror' and persecuted, jailed and executed hundreds of Robespierre sympathizers.

A new (third) constitution was drawn up, the Constitution of 1795. It was approved in a referendum by 95,4% of votes. The constitution installed a bicameral system, while granting the executive power to a Directory, a committee of five people. It guaranteed freedom of religion, press and labour, but forbade public meetings of political societies. Shortly afterwards, a rebellion started against the Thermidorian regime and its constitution, but this was put down with brutal violence by the young general Napoleon.

It must be said that after the constitution was implemented, France saw two years of relative stability supported by military successes abroad. However, in 1797, the Directors started to fight each other. This led to a new coup (18 Fructidor), with new purges and major economic mismanagement. Unnecessary and weak military campaigns motivated an international coalition to invade France again. The fighting Directors had no choice other than to call on Napoleon Bonaparte for help.

4. THE END OF THE REVOLUTION: THE 18TH BRUMAIRE

On 9 November 1799 (the 18th Brumaire on the French calendar), Bonaparte's coup d'état put an end to the Directory and both assemblies. The Constitution of 1795 (the Year III) was abolished and a new Constitution (of the Year VII) adopted, installing a Consulate of three Consuls. In a coup within the coup, Napolean appointed himself First Consul. In a referendum, 99,9% of the voters approved the constitution. In 1802, another referendum confirmed (with 99,8% approval) Napoleon as 'First Consul for Life'. Two years later, the Senate passed a bill abolishing the First Republic and installing the French Empire, with Napoleon as its Emperor.

The rest is well known. France experienced one regime change after another. This lasted until 1870, when the country turned into a stable democracy under the Third Republic. The constitution of 1875 was the 14th constitution since the beginning of the French Revolution 86 years earlier.

A chronology of the Arab Revolution

When Mohamed Bouazizi set himself on fire on 17 December 2010, protests spread across Tunisia. On 14 January 2011, Tunisian president Ben Ali fled to Saudi Arabia. The Arab world was shocked and many wondered if they could obtain a similar result. On 14 January, people started demonstrating in Jordan. On 25 January, the 'Day of the Police', thousands of Egyptians started to fill Tahrir Square. On 11 February, after 18 days of struggle, the Supreme Council of Armed Forces acted on the demands of the people and deposed President Mubarak. On 3 February, protests had started in Yemen. On 17 February in Libya. On 19 February in Bahrain. On 20 February in Morocco. On 14 March in Saudi Arabia. On 15 March in Syria.

The outcome of all these protests differed substantially. In Tunisia, Egypt and Yemen, the revolutions ousted the president in a relatively peaceful manner. In Jordan and Morocco, the protests seemed to fade away after both Kings promised reforms. In Bahrain and Saudi Arabia, demonstrations were crushed. In Libya and Syria, both revolutions led to a full-scale war. Whereas international military intervention helped the revolutionaries in Libya to put an end to the destruction, the devastation in Syria is still going on.

As it is difficult to go into the details of events in every country of the Arab Revolution while keeping a bird's eye perspective, I will focus on the chronology of Egypt's revolution only. Egypt is by far the largest country in the Middle East and North Africa – it has as many citizens as the other countries combined – and, more than any other country, its events have influenced and continue to influence the rest of the region.

I. THE RULE OF THE SUPREME COUNCIL OF ARMED FORCES

After eighteen days of massive protests on Tahrir Square, the Supreme Council of Armed Forces (SCAF) took over the power of President Mubarak. This certainly felt like a honeymoon period, with the people and the army on one side against the old regime on the other. The most hated of the Mubarak era were put behind bars to face trial later. On 19 March 2011, a package with constitutional reforms passed a referendum with 77% voter support. The turnout was 41%. Although there was critique that the reforms didn't go far enough, the package did limit the presidency to two terms and set up a plan of transition towards parliamentary and presidential elections.

The honeymoon period waned as cracks began to show, with several incidents between the revolutionaries and the SCAF: the clashes in Mohamed Mahmud Street, where protesters asked to replace the government; the Maspero incident, in which peacefully protesting Coptic Christians were killed by the police; the clashes at the Cabinet of the Prime Minister; and the football drama in Port Said. There were also cracks inside the revolutionary camp itself: divisions between the revolutionaries of the first hour and the Muslim Brotherhood (MB). The MB had only decided to join the revolution when it became clear this was serious, and it seemed now to take the side of the army.

The first parliamentary elections at the end of 2012 were a success. People queued for hours to cast their vote. One could feel the wind of change and freedom. The Muslim Brotherhood was the big winner, just like their sister party, Ennahda, in Tunisia.

2. THE REIGN OF THE MUSLIM BROTHERHOOD

After the parliamentary elections, the Muslim Brotherhood also won the presidency. Claiming to be the real defenders of the revolution, president Mohamed Morsi started to undo some of the decisions taken by the SCAF. He replaced Field Marshall Tantawi with General Abdel Fatah Sisi as chief of the Armed Forces. Chief editors of newspapers and television channels were replaced, as well as some judges. Fearing a conspiracy or a coup, Morsi took all power in a constitutional decree on 22 November 2012. Massive protests took the streets again.

On 23 December 2012, a new constitution passed a referendum with 63,8% of the votes. The turnout was 32,68%. The constitution had a clear Islamic rubberstamp. People started to fear a kind of Islamic rule would be installed. The president's speeches often sounded like sermons and many people had taken the initiative to ban alcohol in bars or restaurants or to force women to wear the veil. A campaign was launched against leading politicians and media figures who were accused of spying, conspiring, heresy or defaming the Prophet. It made more and more people believe that the real power lied in the hands of the leadership of the Muslim Brotherhood rather than the presidency and that Morsi was not the president of the Egyptians but of the Muslim Brothers. The opposition saw no option but to try and organize a new revolution.

3. THE EGYPTIAN THERMIDOR

A few days before the protest on 30 June 2013, President Morsi gave a long speech live on TV. He accused opposition politicians, the media, the judiciary and supporters of the Mubarak regime of corruption, conspiracy and being paid by foreign hands. He even mentioned names. The effect was to convince many Egyptians that Morsi and the Muslim Brotherhood were indeed a threat. Millions took the street on 30 June in what was probably the largest protest ever in history. Fearing a bloodbath, Army Chief General Sisi confronted Morsi with an ultimatum: he had three days to propose a compromise. Instead, Morsi gave a new speech, rejected the ultimatum and said that he was "willing to spill his own blood". The next day, General Sisi, backed by opposition leader Mohamed El Baradei and the religious leaders of the Coptic Church and Al Azhar[2], announced

---

2   Founded in 970, Al Azhar is – after Fez - the second oldest university in the world. It is seen as the most important centre of Sunni learning, teaching Islamic religion and

that Morsi was no longer president and that a transition period would follow with a new constitution and new elections.

The Muslim Brothers notwithstanding, most Egyptians seemed to be happy with the new government and felt they had regained their freedom. A new constitution was written and approved in a referendum with 98,1% votes of support. The turnout was 38,6%. The new constitution got rid of the Islamic rhetoric of the former constitution. It granted freedom of religion and press. However, in reality, these freedoms were curtailed by a new 'War on Terror'. The Muslim Brotherhood was labelled a terrorist organization and many of its leaders arrested, TV channels and newspapers were closed down and an 'anti-protest law' forbade spontaneous protests and public political meetings. The bloody crackdown triggered terrorist attacks. It inspired many Egyptians to call on General Sisi to take over the country.

4. WILL IT ALL END WITH PRESIDENT SISI?

As I write, General Sisi has been appointed Field Marshall by interim president Adli Mansour. The SCAF has cleared the way so that Sisi can run for the presidency. There is no doubt he will win. After more than three years of struggle, this will not sound good to the world, nor to the revolutionaries. Is this what they have been fighting for?

As mentioned earlier, making historical comparisons can be dangerous and is often based on an oversimplification of events and the logic of events. It would be unfair to compare the first years of the French Revolution with the times of the SCAF. In France, far more radical decisions had been made. Calling Mohamed Morsi the Egyptian Robespierre would be most unjust. Under the French Reign of Terror, no less than 40,000 people were killed, of whom 16.594 by guillotine.

But as Mark Twain said: "History doesn't repeat itself, but it does rhyme." And it must be said that the course of events of both the French and the Egyptian Revolution do rhyme remarkably well. In both France and Egypt, there were three constitutions within a very short period of time. And even if we cannot call the Morsi presidency a real Reign of Terror, it surely was a Reign of Virtue with elements of Terror. Egypt too has seen a Thermidor-type reaction. Though in France this happened in

---

culture. Therefore, Al Azhar is considered as the representative of Sunni Muslims in Egypt.

the Convention, in Egypt it happened in the streets. Both were supported by the army. And both events were followed by a new strongman.

Another point of similarity worth touching on is the 'domino-effect'. Just as the other countries of the Arab world were petrified that the revolution would reach their people, so the rest of Europe was afraid of the consequences of the French Revolution. The revolutionary idea was popping up in the most surprising places. One example is Martinique, then a French colony, where officials received a letter in 1789 that said: "We, the Negroes, know that we are free... We will die for this liberty." In 1791, there was a great slave revolt in another colony, Saint-Domingue, which led to both the abolition of slavery and the establishment of the first state founded by former slaves: Haïti.

The Arab Revolution has gone far, though it is impossible to say at this point in which stage are, for example, Libya or Yemen. And the question of what will happen in Syria or what might still happen in Saudi Arabia remains. These questions cannot be answered by merely concentrating on a chronology of events. In order to understand more deeply, we should delve into the ideas that shaped both revolutions. Here lies the answer to where the 'Enlightenment' can be found in the Arab Revolution.

The ideas of the French Revolution

It is common knowledge that it were the ideas of the Enlightenment that inspired the French Revolution. Philosophers like Baruch de Spinoza, John Locke, Pierre Bayle, Voltaire and physicist Isaac Newton triggered this great intellectual change. The Enlightenment culminated in *l'Encyclopédie* of Denis Diderot and Jean le Rond d'Alembert, with its contributions from hundreds of leading intellectuals like Voltaire, Jean-Jacques Rousseau and Montesquieu. The ideas were spread all over Europe and the United States.

In his 1784 essay, 'What is Enlightenment?', Immanuel Kant gives the following definition: "Enlightenment is man's emergence from his self-imposed nonage. Nonage is the inability to use one's own understanding without another's guidance. This nonage is self-imposed if its cause lies not in lack of understanding but in indecision and lack of courage to use one's own mind without another's guidance. Dare to know! Sapere aude. 'Have the courage to use your own understanding,' is therefore the motto of the enlightenment."

Dorinda Outram, in *The Enlightenment* (1995), describes it this way: "Enlightenment was a desire for human affairs to be guided by rationality rather than by faith, superstition, or revelation; a belief in the power of human reason to change society and liberate the individual from the restraints of custom or arbitrary authority; all backed up by a world view increasingly validated by science rather than by religion or tradition."

However, the question we are asking ourselves in this context is not primarily what Enlightenment is, but why was it so strong in France and why did it lead to a revolution? The answer takes us back to 1685, or the Revocation of the Edict of Nantes. The Edict of Nantes, issued in 1598 by Henry IV of France, had granted the French Calvinists (the Huguenots) important rights. It marked the end of the religious wars in France following the Reformation. The revocation of this edict by Louis XIV made France a Catholic state again and the Huguenots thus heretics. This resulted in an exodus of Huguenots, mainly to the neighbouring countries of Britain, the Netherlands and Switzerland.

Obviously, these Huguenots were angry with France, its monarchy and its Catholicism. They wanted a tolerant France with freedom of religion and freedom of speech. Britain's Glorious Revolution had already brought these freedoms and a parliamentary system; it is no surprise that the Enlightenment's flag was flying high here. The Netherlands was in its Golden Age and one of the most tolerant countries on earth; no wonder Pierre Bayle, one of the first French Enlightenment thinkers, lived there. Geneva was then a Calvinist city. It was there that Jean-Jacques Rousseau lived and shaped his ideas.

The Huguenots translated the most interesting and revolutionary English books into French, published them (mainly in the Netherlands) and smuggled them into France. The same happened from Switzerland. Not only great ideas were smuggled in. Pamphlets against the King of France, making a fool of him, were secretly brought in, and many people read them. The combination of the two created a pre-revolutionary atmosphere and fertile ground for more extreme ideas once the revolution had started.

The ideas of the Arab Revolution

The Arab world has known its own Revocation of the Edict of Nantes, but in the opposite way. During the First World War, the Arabs were convinced by the British to cooperate and chase the Ottomans out of the

Arab domain. We all know the story of Lawrence of Arabia. They were promised their own state, with the Hashemites as its kings. Although they did succeed in pushing the Ottomans back into what is currently Turkey, the French and the British signed the secret Sykes–Picot Agreement and divided the Middle East between them. Not only did the Europeans betray their Arab allies, they also agreed on creating a new home for the Jews in Palestine.

However, a much bigger shock was still to come. The new leader of Turkey, Kemal Atatürk, abolished the Ottoman Empire and the Sultanate and, in 1924, the Turkish Parliament abolished the Caliphate. Even though the Caliphate's authority was no longer that significant, this was the first time since the Prophet Mohamed – the first time in 1,400 years – that the Sunni Muslims did not have a Caliph or successor of the Prophet to lead the Islamic world.

Shortly afterwards, in 1928, a teacher in Egypt, Hassan Al Banna, started a new movement: the Muslim Brotherhood. The goal was clear: getting rid of the impious and treacherous Western occupiers and reinstalling the Caliphate. The means to reach these goals were initially to convince the people of Egypt to reject Western influences and become 'better Muslims'. One way to convince them was to organize a social solidarity system under its members. It was a very successful movement, spreading quickly in Egypt and all over the Muslim world.

It is obvious that the rulers of Egypt and other countries didn't like this ideological movement directed against them and organized as a state within the state. Since the very beginning there has been a fight between the state and the Muslim Brotherhood, resulting in assassinations and attacks. Hassan Al Banna himself was assassinated. In many countries, the Muslim Brotherhood was forbidden and crushed. But as an underground organization, they were well organized – and started to become more radical with thinkers like Sayed Qutb. His writings inspired Osama Bin Laden and the current leader of Al Qaeda, Ayman Al Zawahiri, a former member of the Muslim Brotherhood. Their hatred is directed against the dictators supported by the West. Their goal is to reinstall the Caliphate. Hence their slogan "Islam is the solution". This is why so many Egyptians feared that Mohamed Morsi and the Muslim Brotherhood would not organize free elections ever again. People started to understand that the Muslim Brothers were convinced that this was their moment to realize their dreams. They failed and the masses on the streets in Egypt on 30 June 2013 show that there is another important current of ideas.

This current has its roots in the French Revolution or, more precisely, in the year 1798, when Napoleon Bonaparte invaded Egypt. The entire Arab world witnessed its stagnation while, on the other side of the Mediterranean, culture and science had been advancing. This cultural shock brought back memories of the times when the Arab world was at its most glorious: the era of the Caliphate in Baghdad. From the 8th to 10th centuries, all great Greek, Persian and Indian works of philosophy and science were translated into Arabic. This was the basis for great scientific inventions in mathematics, chemistry, medicine, astronomy and, later, history, philosophy and sociology. This era was funded by the Mu'tazilah movement of intellectuals promoting a separation between religion and science.

It was this philosophy of using (not copying) great ideas from other cultures that inspired the Al Nahda (Renaissance) in Egypt and Syria. This movement started in 1826 when the Egyptian ruler Mohamed Ali sent Rifa'a Al Tahtawi to study in Paris. Five years later, Tahtawi returned with a positive view of France. He translated many important scientific and literary works into Arabic. In his opinion, the Arabic world should be reformed, adapting ideas of the West to the Islamic culture.

The Al Nahda has a mixed legacy. The Muslim Brotherhood used the ideas of one of Al Nahda's religious thinkers, Sayyid Jamal-al-Din Afghani, to propagate Islamic unity against the West and to promote their own Ennahda project. Nevertheless, the most important current coming out of Al Nahda was clearly a secular one. Indeed, the Egyptian writer Taha Houssein (1889–1973), who is seen as the last great representative of the Al Nahda movement, was an atheist.

What we are seeing in the Arab Revolution is a deep clash between those who believe that "Islam is the solution" and those who believe that "Islam should be separated from politics and science". This is a clash with 1,200-year-old roots. It is a battle between a closed society and an open society not afraid to look over the fence for new ideas. The Enlightenment started with people looking over the fence. In the 17th century, books about travels to Egypt, Turkey, Persia, India and China caused people like Pierre Bayle to doubt the "dogmatic rightness" of their own society. Both the Enlightenment and Al Nahda were first questioning and then fighting a deeply religious, conservative and dogmatic society.

Why the French Revolution succeeded – and why the Arab Revolution will too

Although we can say that the French Revolution ended with Napoleon's coup d'état in 1799, its ideas and ideals certainly didn't die on the 18th Brumaire. On the contrary, they remain the subject of ongoing philosophical battles. There were three reasons why the French Revolution finally succeeded.

The first is that its ideas were spread during a communication revolution. Around 1750, three centuries after the invention of printing, the amount of published books exploded. New to the 18th century was the use of pamphlets, a popular way of spreading criticism and ideas (famous pamphlet writers include Voltaire and Mirabeau). The history of newspapers and their role in the spreading of ideas during the French revolution are even more fascinating. The first newspaper of France, La Gazette, started to be printed in 1631. It was a weekly newspaper that played the role of mouthpiece of the King. In 1789, La Gazette even did not report the storming of the Bastille. Because of the censorship, all other, later newspapers focused not on politics but on culture. There were Huguenot newspapers criticizing the politics of France, but these were printed in Switzerland, The Netherlands or Germany and brought to French readers in clandestine ways. Only in 1777, the first daily newspaper, le Journal de Paris, appeared in France.

After the fall of the Bastille, the French press changed dramatically. Every revolutionary who wanted to be taken seriously had his own newspaper. During the French Revolution, there were no less than 80 newspapers. The most famous ones were *L'Ami du peuple* of Jean-Paul Marat, *Le Tribun du Peuple* of Gracchus Babeuf and *La Tribune des patriotes* of Camille Desmoulins. They did no longer talk about culture but about political events and ideas. It was during the French Revolution that newspapers were sold in the streets of Paris for the first time. This communication revolution made the spreading of ideas fast and efficient. The French revolutionaries transformed an existing communication tool with low impact into an important political tool.

The second reason the French revolution succeeded is that it surfed on the wave of the Industrial Revolution. In 1789, the Industrial Revolution had not reached the European continent yet. France was mainly an agricultural country. Although Britain was far ahead in its industrialization process. Paris made a free-trade treaty with London in

1786, the Eden-Treaty. As the French industries were no match to the British, manufactories collapsed all over northern France. In 1787-1789, half a million people lost their income. It was one important element that created the anger that lead to the French Revolution.

The Industrial Revolution played also a crucial role in the spreading of the French revolutionary ideas. One example is Belgium, that became independent in 1830. It adopted a constitution based on the Declaration of Human Rights and of the Citizen and started immediately with its industrialization. Other European countries that industrialized but did not adopt these revolutionary ideas faced a European-wide revolution in 1848. The economical revolution went hand in hand with a political revolution, with many ups and downs until deep in the 20th century.

The third reason is a growth in the size of the population and, with it, changed demographics. When France went from 20 to 30 million citizens in one century, there was an excess of ambitious and frustrated young people. This group would only grow further in the century to come. These are the people that need change in order to move forward and have a future of their own.

Today in the Arab world, these three conditions are present. A communication revolution is under way. The Internet and social media are thoroughly changing the way people are interacting. But more importantly, these channels are very strong and quick carriers of ideas. Calling the Arab Revolution a Facebook revolution would be akin to calling the French Revolution a Newspaper revolution: absurd. The pamphlet and newspaper writers of the French Revolution are the bloggers and social media users of the Arab Revolution. They too turned a communication tool with a limited political impact into a powerful and uncontrollable political tool. The same happened during protests in Brazil, Venezuala, Ukraine and Mexico. It is clear that the role of both Facebook and Twitter and its successors since 2011 as intellectual and political tools is undeniable and their influence will continue to grow in the years to come.

Also undeniable is the fact that we are facing a new economic revolution. Some call it the Third Industrial Revolution, others the Third Wave or the Network Society. In any case, we live in a new economic framework that will carry a new framework of ideas.

Thirdly, the demographics in the Arab world are rapidly changing. Today, more than half of the population is younger than 25 and this group will only grow in the decades to come. Arab society is still deeply conservative and patriarchal, blocking the ambitions and dreams of millions of young people. The revolt of the young will change this society and the role of its religion, for this is the only way to acquire the future they are dreaming of.

Conclusion

It took France fourteen constitutions and 86 years to progress from the start of its revolution to the stable democracy of the Third Republic in 1875. It took a very messy and bloody start and made France, and Europe, an unstable region for a long time. But the revolution changed the world as we knew it. It changed our political system, our way of thinking and the way we deal with the relationship between state and religion.

The Arab Revolution is now three years old, The situation is indeed messy and bloody. There is no doubt that the Middle East and Northern Africa will remain unstable for many years to come. It is unclear what will happen in Syria, Algeria, Palestine, Saudi Arabia and even Iran. What transpires in each of these countries will have a major impact on the rest of the Arab world. We will see an ongoing battle between the conservatives and the progressives, between those who believe Islam is the solution and those who don't.

However, calling this already an Arab Winter or a failed Arab Spring is shortsighted to say the least. What is going on in the Arab world is a true Revolution. I can only hope that I have succeeded in convincing the reader that the 'Arab Spring' has all the characteristics of a real – and important – revolution. So let us allow the Arab world more time to become a stable, free and democratic region.

III

Inside the Arab Revolution
Three Years of Publishing

Before I went to live in the Arab world I didn't understand why anyone would write a blog. A blog, I thought, is basically an opinion piece published on a random page on the Internet. So how would anyone read this piece? And if nobody finds the piece, why go through the effort of writing it? Another thing I didn't understand much was the power of social media. I didn't find it interesting to read what people were doing or feeling at every moment of the day. It all seemed a waste of time and energy.

When I arrived in Cairo in September 2011 however, it was only a matter of days before the significance of social media became clear to me. Most activists hardly communicate via telephone. They 'talk' via Twitter, organize via Facebook and air opinions via blog posts. Social media isn't social, but *political*. Revolutionaries write an opinion on a blog and spread it via their huge Twitter and Facebook networks, which have an enormous multiplication effect. If someone with hundred thousand followers on Twitter tweets your blog post, it is going around. I suddenly realized that Twitter (and Facebook) are incredibly effective tools to spread opinion, make news and follow the most interesting articles from all over the world.

A conversation I had with the publisher of *Al Masri Al Youm*, the biggest Egyptian newspaper, made me realize how far behind most European newspapers are on the social media front. Too many newspapers don't even make their opinion pages available on their website. They send you a PDF file with which you can do nothing on Twitter. Arab media have large teams to spread and promote their published pieces, both in Arabic and in English. Those who are best at doing this attract the best writers and the biggest names.

So I started blogging to spread my pieces as much as possible, obtain more followers on Twitter and, in this way, become an opinion actor. It is another way of doing politics – and it is the only way to influence the complex debate in the Arab world.

I failed more times than I succeeded. But on the occasions you succeed, things get really big. I was stunned to see how a few pieces were immediately translated into Arabic and started to live their own life. As you will see shortly, one piece was discussed on prime time Egyptian TV three evenings in a row. In one of the evenings Mohamed Morsi, then one of the two remaining presidential candidates of Egypt, was forced by the anchor to agree with my proposals, 45 minutes long. I was equally surprised to see another blog post shared more than 19,000 times on Facebook. It was even transformed into a leaflet. And one of my pieces on the Free Syrian Army has been republished on so many websites that I am simply unable to follow it anymore.

Social media is not social in the Arab world; it is a political weapon that can build and destroy. President Morsi announced the cancellation of a tax law at 3 am on his Facebook profile 12 hours after it had been issued because too many people attacked the law on Twitter. One day after the mass demonstrations of 30 June 2013, the Muslim Brotherhood tested the idea of a referendum on the Egyptian presidency on Twitter and understood it wouldn't bring the solution they were hoping for. The Syrian war is being waged half on the ground and half on social media, while one Tunisian minister almost had to resign after an accusation on Facebook.

People in the Arab world don't trust the mainstream media anymore. Too often newspapers and TV channels have been used as propaganda tools of the powers that be. The result is that citizens trust more what their friends say on social media than what appears in the media. The credibility of news depends more and more on the credibility of the source.

Building credibility takes a long time, while you can lose it in a matter of minutes. Therefore, a good blog post needs to contain information based on strong sources. It has to take sides, but only through good arguments. And it must add something new to the debate. If these conditions are met, a single blog post can – with a bit of luck – change the hearts and minds of many and eventually change their politics.

A number of people told me that if Morsi had followed the proposal in one of my aforementioned blogs, the June 2013 protests would not have happened. Others claim that my pieces on the Free Syrian Army changed the way Washington looked at the FSA and its general commander Salim Idriss. It is impossible for me to verify this, but I would of course be most honoured if I played even the slightest role.

The following pages give an overview of the blogs and articles I published over the past three years. I have chosen not to make a selection, even though some of the pieces are slightly outdated, too naive or even premature. As a historian I think it might be interesting to follow the mindset of an observer during the course of this time, with both its optimism and frustrations, hope and despair, successes and failures. In any case, this approach provides the reader with an honest overview of three years of publishing about the Arab Revolution.

EGYPT
Reflections from October 2011
to September 2013

Blogging in Egypt about Egypt can be a dangerous hobby. Under Hosni Mubarak, President from 1981 to 2011, most bloggers used a pseudonym and wrote from anonymous locations online. One Internet activist, Khaled Said, was discovered and beaten to death in Alexandria on 6 June 2010 after he posted a video on the Internet of officers sharing the spoils from a drug bust. The pictures of Said's deformed face became a symbol of Egypt's police brutality and motivated one young Egyptian citizen, Wael Ghonim, to start the Facebook page 'We are all Khaled Said'.

After the revolution of January 2011 and the resignation of Mubarak, most writers behind the anonymous blogs went public and became well-known activists. However, that doesn't mean they were left in peace. Critical voices continue to be accused of being foreign-funded agents of the West or spies, of defamation of the presidency, the Prophet and Islam, or of conspiring against Egypt.

As a foreigner in Egypt one has to be careful as well. Authorities can make your life difficult. One tactic is to make you wait for months for a working and/or residence permit. Before the presidential elections of 2012, the Supreme Council of Armed Forces even ran a TV advertisement warning Egyptians: foreigners might look kind but many of them are spies. This is perhaps why a good Egyptian friend called me in the middle of the night begging me to delete one of my blog posts as "they might come after me".

Another good friend, Ahmed Maher, was accused of breaking the anti-protest law. This law is issued in November 2013 and forbids unapproved gatherings in the street of more than ten people. Ahmed is the leader of the April 6 Youth Movement. It was this movement that organized the revolution of 25 January 2011. They asked the Egyptians to go to Tahrir Square that day and start a peaceful sit-in. One of their leaders, Asmaa Mahfouz, received the Sakharov Price of the European Parliament as a recognition for the key role the April 6 Youth Movement played in the revolution in Egypt and the Arab revolution in general. After his sentence, Ahmed is writing letters from jail, criticizing the repressive climate in Egypt. He is writing in secret on toilet paper as in prison they refuse him pen and paper.

All this nervousness must mean that blog posts do influence political debate in Egypt. Bloggers like Mahmoud Salem (Sandmonkey), Mona

Elthahawy, Bassem Sabry (An Arab Citizen), Wael Abbas (Arabdigital), Zeinobia (still anonymous), Sarah Carr, Maikel Nabil and many others continue to be the intellectual revolutionaries playing the conscience of Egyptian society. It is nearly impossible to understand what is going on in Egypt without reading their analyses.

After the revolution of 2011 the Egyptian train of history has been speeding like never before. Not one day has gone by without someone being killed or arrested or standing trial; without a party being started or falling apart; without demonstrations demanding either the government or the president to resign. Since 2011 Egypt has had two revolutions, three constitutions, four presidents and five prime ministers.

It is not easy to understand what is happening. Divided as Egypt is, politics is a matter of life and death. I have seen many people fighting for freedom, while knowing the risk. Many have been killed. This makes it hard sometimes to stay objective and impossible to remain neutral. But the purpose of my mission in Egypt was never neutrality. As a representative of the Liberal and Democrat Group in the European Parliament, my mission was to stand behind those who fight for freedom, liberal democracy and human rights.

Egyptians are proud and therefore unwilling to take advice from foreigners. It is possible to get their attention only if you leave your European attitude of 'we know better' behind. At a certain point I started to use the phrase "An outsider's perspective" in my blog and article titles, giving the message that I do realize that my point of view has some limitations. And I have always asked at least one Egyptian to read my pieces before I published in order to be sure that I would not make any big mistakes. Here are the 18 pieces that went ahead and were published.

1. There is no problem with the Copts ...
Published on *EU Observer*, 12 October 2011

On the night of 9 October 2011, a group of Coptic Christians demonstrated at Maspero, the Egyptian State media headquarters in Cairo, not far from Tahrir Square. They demanded a reaction from the government against attacks on churches. Suddenly, armoured police vehicles drove into the crowd at high speed, some shooting at protestors. At the same time, State TV announced that the army was under attack and that citizens should go out and defend the soldiers. 28 people were killed and 212 injured that night.

On Monday (10 October) I received a message from a friend, a "true Muslima" as she calls herself. It read: "Two of my friends died last night. I am breaking down. One of them was to get married in a couple of months. His friends sent me a picture of his fiancée holding his dead body. Mubarak was a curtain, SCAF is the monster we unveiled!"

This is just one of the many messages of despair I received after Sunday's events. A peaceful demonstration of Copts in the evening was interrupted by unknown people throwing stones at the demonstrators. Half an hour later, soldiers arrived, together with the police, and started a brutal crackdown. Firing live bullets, driving tanks into crowds. Leaving behind 24 dead and 150 wounded. One dozen people died under the wheels of a tank. The pictures are very disturbing.

Why? The Copts were demonstrating peacefully against the fact that the Supreme Council of Armed Forces (SCAF) is not reacting appropriately to attacks on Coptic churches. Not life-threatening to a government, is it? Moreover, there are demonstrations here every week. No wonder then that a lot of questions and theories are popping up. Why have last week's attackers of the Coptic Church in the region of Aswan not been brought to court? This is a valid question, certainly if you know that since February this year already 12,000 people have been sentenced by military court for disturbing the public order. This was not a massive attack. Only a dozen Salafis (Muslim extremists) sacked the little church, unaware that someone was filming them. The fact that one of the guys on camera was not a Salafi but an officer from the Ministry of Interior did of course lead to an explosion of conspiracy theories.

One of the most popular theories among Egyptians at the moment is that the SCAF is organising these attacks and this chaos in order to keep power and maintain the emergency law and military courts[1]. In any case, what happened on Sunday will not diminish the doubts about the real intentions of the military. As my friend's text message implied, the fact that it is still not clear when the presidential elections are going to be held and when the power of the SCAF will be transferred to a civilian doesn't help either.

There remains the question about the situation of the Copts in Egypt. Until last weekend, my friend (whose name I deliberately don't mention) told me that there are no problems with the Copts. A message I have heard many, many times. And although a monk at the Coptic Monastery of Saint Anthony, one of the oldest abbies in the world, told me a different story two days ago, everybody must admit that attacks on churches are being carried out by a few persons only but condemned by everyone – including the Muslim Brotherhood. It is true that the Copts do face challenges as a minority[2], but what happened yesterday can't be reduced to a 'Coptic problem'.

There are two possible conclusions: either the situation after the revolution has become more chaotic and has given extremists new opportunities, or someone is deliberately trying to create chaos and frictions between religious groups. Either way, the military bears some responsibility. And if the SCAF doesn't take its responsibility seriously to safeguard the revolution, I predict a new revolution in Egypt in the months to come.

---

1   The Emergency Law in Egypt was imposed during the 1967 war against Israel. It ended in 1980, but was reimposed after the assassination of President Anwar Sadat in 1981. The state of emergency expired on 31 May 2012. The law gave the police extended power; it suspended constitutional rights and enforced heavy censorship. Military trials are a way of sentencing people without a proper process or a proper defense.
2   Egypt has one of the earliest churches in the world. It was founded by Saint Mark in the first century AD. After the Council of Chalcedon in 451 the Coptic Church broke away from the Orthodox Church, becoming an independent Egyptian Church. Egypt was one of the first countries taken in the Muslim conquest in 639. Since then Coptic Christians have slowly become a minority. Today it is estimated that 10 percent of the Egyptians are Coptic Christians.

2. Towards a second Egyptian revolution
Published on *EU Observer*, 20 November 2011

On 18 November 2011 there was a big but quiet demonstration on Tahrir Square, which I attended with my family. Some 200 activists decided to stay overnight on the square and continue on to the next day. In the early morning of 20 November, police broke up the tents and deployed teargas. It was the beginning of the clashes in Mohamed Mahmoud Street, bordering the square. More than 40 people were killed and many lost an eye (police targeted the eyes with plastic bullets). This marked the first real crisis of the rule of the Supreme Council of Armed Forces.

When I woke up this morning, a strange fog was hanging over my neighbourhood. It smelled like something was burning, but different. Only after I entered Tahrir Square, did I realise it was a cloud of tear gas. On Tahrir, it was impossible to keep your eyes dry. Every five minutes, tear gas was being shot into the crowds. New and better equipment, activists told me, with the label 'Made in the USA'. It is hard to think of a more efficient way for our American friends to destroy their already fragile image... What happened on Tahrir to create a fog of teargas that extended miles from the city?

Last night [19 November], I received a lot of panicky messages from friends who were on the square. In the morning, the police cleared the square in a brutal way. There was no reason for this violence as protesters were merely sleeping in their tents. After that, security forces started on a severe crackdown in which a few thousand people were injured and two killed.

This is not the first time that the military has cleared Tahrir Square for security reasons. It is after all a major crossroad in Cairo. But this time the people aren't accepting it. It is the army that refuses to abolish the emergency law and military trials, in which more than 12,000 people have been sentenced. It is the army that delayed clarifying the electoral process. It is the army that wants to have 'extra-constitutional rights' by which their budget would stay secret and by which they could cancel any law adopted by Parliament. And last but not least, it is the army that refuses to set a date for the presidential elections, which would end military rule. And today the Supreme Council announced they would hand over their power by the end of 2012 *if* (!) the chaos would end.

The Egyptian people didn't risk their lives to end the rule of Mubarak and get another military regime in his place. That is why they are angry and why they won't leave Tahrir that easily anymore. Many even talk about a second revolution in order to obtain real democracy. Are we witnessing the start of this second revolution? It is hard to predict. But one sign in this direction might be that, whereas the mass demonstration of 18 November was dominated by the Muslim Brotherhood, I witness right now that Tahrir is filled again with young and secular activists, the ones who were at the heart of the first revolution on 25 January. The EU should take note too and be quicker than they were during the first revolution to support the demonstrators and their demand for freedom, democracy and the end of the military rule without delay.

3. In bitter fight, Egyptian Islamists rig the elections
Published on *EU Observer*, 14 December 2011

During the first parliamentary elections after the January revolution, it was clear that the Freedom and Justice Party of the Muslim Brotherhood would come out on top. Despite that, they found it necessary not to follow the electoral rules. The main enemies of the Muslim Brotherhood were not the liberal parties but El Nour, the party of the even more conservative Islamists, the Salafis, which was performing much better than expected in the first elections on 28 November 2011. This fight continues today and is the reason why the Salafis backed the army in deposing President Mohamed Morsi on 3 July 2013.

The Muslim Brothers and the Salafis have three things in common. Firstly, both are in favour of political Islam. Secondly, both the Muslim Brothers and the Salafis were surprised by their own successes in the first elections in Egypt. And these two commonalities are why – thirdly – they deeply hate each other.

The Egyptian elections are organised in three phases. In each phase, nine governorates[1] vote for party lists and for independent candidates. The independent candidates must have an absolute majority in order to be elected, which means a second round in most cases. By the first phase of the elections of 28 November, the Freedom and Justice Party of the Muslim Brotherhood had 40 percent of the votes, the Salafis a surprising 24 percent in the most liberal governorates of Egypt.

Now (on 14–15 December) Egyptians have to vote in nine other – more conservative – governorates. The political battle is no longer about an Islamic or a liberal state. It is clearly a brutal confrontation between the Muslim Brothers and the more extreme Salafis. That would be no problem, at least not a democratic one, if both parties would not use all possible means to gain votes. Some examples of reported incidents of fraud:

---

1   Egypt is divided into 27 administrative governorates. Governors are appointed; most of them are retired army generals. For organizational reasons elections are spread over three different phases. In each phase elections are held in nine governorates. Cairo is split in two governorates: Giza and Cairo, both situated on opposite sides of the Nile.

- In Suez, a judge (who is supervising the elections there) was seen signing ballot papers for voters, voting for El-Nour.
- Also in Suez, Salafis were attempting to convince voters waiting in long lines to vote for them. Activists who were filming this forbidden campaigning have been arrested.
- In another polling station in Suez, voters were not allowed to put their ballot paper into the ballot box themselves.
- In Gerla-Sohag, a huge banner of El-Nour was hanging above the entrance of the polling station.
- In Giza (a more liberal area), a polling station has been closed down after there was gunfire around a very calm queue of voters.

This is just a limited list of irregularities, which, in true democratic elections, would result in new, better organised elections being arranged, at least for those areas where the game wasn't played by the rules. It is already clear that in the next few days a long list of electoral frauds will become public. There goes the illusion of so many Egyptians that the most conservative Muslims are also the most honest people. But more important is: what will be the consequence?

A couple of days ago, Egyptian writer Alaa Al-Aswany told me that the military is operating according to double standards. Where the liberals and revolutionaries have to follow the law scrupulously, the Islamist parties can pretty much do whatever they want. He said that the liberal side has been accused of being funded by foreign money (which they have not been), while nothing is done about the proven payment of 300 million Egyptian pounds by someone in the Gulf to an Islamist party. The minister who made this payment public told the press he had forgotten to whom it was paid.

The liberal parties are not, however, losing the elections only because of this kind of fraud on the part of the Islamists. The liberals are too divided to be strong and their campaign is almost solely concentrated on being *against* the Islamist parties instead of promoting their own plans for the future of Egypt. But if Egypt wants to be called a democracy, the rule of law must apply to all parties. At this stage, the Supreme Council of Armed Forces prefers the rule that all parties are equal but some are more equal than others.

4. From Twitter Revolution to Twitter Democracy
Published on *EU Observer*, 30 January 2012

Last week, I saw on Twitter and Facebook what resembled the lead up to the Egyptian revolution last year. On Twitter there was a massive flow of practical information. About every minute, one could follow where exactly which march would be in the next couple of minutes. @Tareqramadan: "Mostafa Mahmoud march now heading towards Dokki Square". If you wanted to join the march heading for Tahrir, you knew exactly where to go to. Or @Askarkazeboon: "Kazeboon 20 January Helwan, facebook.com/events/…", signalling the airing of a documentary intended to show that the military leaders are liars (*kazeboon*) and referring citizens to Facebook for more details on the event.

This was exactly the way it worked during the 18 days of revolution in Egypt in 2011. Facebook was used for general appeals and overviews with information, while the minute-to-minute organisation happened via Twitter. It was on Facebook that Wael Ghonim called for a demonstration on 25 January and that Asmaa Mahfouz posted a video saying that only cowards would not go to Tahrir that day. It was on Twitter, however, that the field hospitals and its supplies were organised and where people were warned about snipers on certain buildings or attacks by thugs in certain parts of the square. One year after Mubarak was toppled, we see again a million people on Tahrir. Not only to celebrate this huge accomplishment of the Egyptian people, but also to demand more progress. The Egyptian revolutionaries are convinced that the revolution is not over. The vast turnout day after day proves social media still works as a tool to continue the revolution.

Since a few months ago, Egyptians have been writing a new chapter of their Twitter history. Twitter is not only being used to organise a revolution, but also to control the result of that revolution: democracy. During the elections for the People's Assembly, Twitter was used all over the country to report violations and fraud. As independent electoral observation was refused by the government, these tweets counted as the most reliable source of information. The days after the elections signaled the start of an even more fascinating story. Since 23 January, tens of thousands of Egyptians have been watching the sessions of the newly elected parliament. Whenever a Member of Parliament says something 'good' or 'bad', it is all around Twitter. Or as @Mostafa wrote: "The public has the right to know what each MP says about each and every bit". Is one MP taking a quick nap? The next minute a picture of his little moment of weakness is all over the Internet.

In a parliamentary democracy, the people are asked once every four years to give their opinion. In a Twitter democracy, citizens applaud and criticise whenever *they* decide to do so. And, as almost all Egyptian politicians are on Twitter, they feel the pressure from the citizens every single moment. They realize that not walking the path to a real Egyptian democracy will immediately lead to a new revolution on Tahrir. The Athenian politician Pericles could never have expected that his famous phrase "the citizens are well capable of judging public affairs" would become reality through Twitter in Egypt.

5. Are the Muslim Brothers Muslim Republicans?

Published on *EU Observer*, 23 February 2012

This piece appears to be the most controversial I have written about the Egyptian revolution and its aftermath. I compared the Muslim Brothers with the American Republicans to show that, even though Europeans shake their heads when they listen to Republican rhetoric, they find a way to give some of the extreme Republican views a place, but cannot do so for the Muslim Brothers. The reason is obvious: we can deal with extreme conservative Christians, but don't know what to make of extreme conservative Muslims. If a Christian like Breivik kills tens of people in Norway, we call him a madman. If a Muslim kills tens of people, we call him a Muslim terrorist. With this blog I was asking that Europe at least give the Muslim Brotherhood a chance, as they were democratically elected – even if it became clear after a few months that they were not about to follow through on their promises. They had the opportunity to become an Egyptian AKP, the moderate Islamist party in Turkey, but have, unfortunately, chosen the other route.

One year after the revolutions in Tunisia, Libya and Egypt, it is clear that the Muslim Brotherhood is poised to become the driving force in Middle Eastern politics. Many in the West are convinced this is the worst possible outcome of the Arab Spring – which some commentators have already nicknamed 'the Arab Winter'. Living in Cairo, I follow the Tunisian and Egyptian elections during the day. At night I watch debates and results from the GOP (Republican) primaries. And frankly, I wonder: is the rhetoric of the MB all that different from that of the primaries?

On their website the Muslim Brotherhood call themselves "a group established to promote development, progress and advancement based on Islamic references". They remain unclear on what exactly these Islamic references are and how their politics will be based on them. The Brothers insist that they will not impose anything on anyone. At most they want to convince their compatriots that living along Islamic principles is preferable. It's worth noting that this stance is less far-reaching than the 30-year-old section of article 2 of the Egyptian constitution – introduced by Mubarak – which says that "Sharia is a principal source of legislation".

When I talk to leading figures of the Brotherhood in Tunisia or Egypt, they seem to agree on a few principles: they want to fix the economy and fight against corruption. I have not heard one of them utter the words 'Islam' or 'Muslim'. In fact, the Brotherhood's vision as written down by Mohamed Morsi, the leader of the Freedom and Justice Party (the Egyptian political wing of the Brotherhood), could be the programme of almost any centrist party in the world. Of course, this is precisely what makes the West suspicious. Is what we see, what we will get?

We seem almost relieved to hear that at least one Brotherhood candidate lives up to the caricature of extremism: she was campaigning on a platform of 'sin-free holidays' in Egypt. Westerners, she posits, are already drinking enough at home and will enjoy two weeks of alcohol- and bikini-free vacations. In the same vein, it's almost reassuring that Hamas is referring to the Egyptian Muslim Brotherhood as their "mother movement", because it provides 'proof' of an international conspiracy against Israel. And didn't the movement officially declare that it wants to "discourage less ethical movies", because "experts suggest that pornography desensitizes men sexually"?

But then the word 'desensitize' suddenly rings a bell. Didn't Michele Bachmann warn that *The Lion King* was the normalization of gayness through desensitization? Didn't Rick Santorum talk about a conscious effort on the part of the left to influence the curriculum to desensitize America to what American values are? It's not the only strange opinion the GOP primaries have telecast. What about Rick Perry saying that Turkey is ruled by Muslim fundamentalists and should be kicked out of NATO? And Newt Gingrich, who went on record saying the Palestinians are an invented people...[1] I wonder how the world would react if an Arab politician called the Israelis an invented people?

And then I remember that day in 2005 when I followed for one day the campaign of House Representative Robert Aderholt in the north of Alabama. I was surprised when, in those dry counties of the Bible belt, I heard the sentence that I hear so often in Egypt today: "Sorry, but we serve no alcohol, sir." Alderholt's main fight was trying to display the Ten Commandments in every public building. When quizzed about it, he quoted Reagan, who apparently once said that "we might come closer to

---

[1] Michelle Bachmann, Rick Santorum, Rick Perry and Newt Gingrich were candidates for the nomination of the Republican Party for the American presidential elections of 2012.

balancing the budget if all of us live closer to the Ten Commandments and the Golden Rule".

For a European, it's almost incomprehensible how politics and religion intermingle in US elections. The Republican aversion against the very essence of the European social welfare state puzzles me. Also, the consensus between GOP candidates that the US needs to bomb Iran seemed to confirm the European cliché that American politicians are addicted to the drumbeat of war.

But although I can't understand the GOP on an emotional level, I'm not afraid of them. It's clear to me that however unfathomable their politics are, they believe in the process of democracy. Maybe the Muslim Brotherhood is just like the Republican Party in that regard. They might be hard to understand, but still be democrats. I hope that if they come to power, the Republicans will deliver less of what they say. And I hope the Brotherhood will not deliver more than what they promise. But I do think that, just as the United States does, Egypt should have the right to have a democratic, religious conservative party.

6. Elections in Egypt: some early conclusions
Published on *EU Observer*, 24 May 2012

Today, just as yesterday, millions of Egyptians are casting their vote in the first democratic presidential elections ever. Already since 5 am, men and women have been waiting in line in front of the polling stations. Around 8 am, I saw thousands of people quietly standing in lines of hundreds of metres, hoping to seal the change Egypt has been going through since the revolution of beginning 2011. For many weeks and even months, Egyptians have been discussing these elections all the time and everywhere. The first question people have been asking each other in metro, taxi or teahouse is always: who are you going to vote for? Without doubt, the most remarkable moment of the presidential campaign was the debate, live on two commercial television stations, between Amr Moussa and Abdel Moneim Aboul Fotouh, the two top contenders for the presidency. The debate lasted for four and a half hours, until two o'clock at night. Pubs were packed with people cheering the debate as if it was the finale of the Champions League. It is very clear: Egyptians adore free elections and no one is going to take this away from them.

Although today is only the beginning of the presidential process – on 16–17 June there is the second round and on 30 June the transfer of power –, some conclusions can already be drawn:

1. These elections are democratic because the outcome is totally unpredictable. Where three weeks ago everybody would have said that Moussa and Aboul Fotouh would go to the second round, today it is impossible to make a prediction. There are five top candidates and every single one of them has the possibility of winning.

> (1) Amr Moussa (former foreign minister of Mubarak and former secretary-general of the Arab League) started his campaign almost the day after Mubarak was ousted from office. Moussa is popular because he talks like the people in the street do. Some even call him populist. His advantage is his experience, his disadvantage his links to the old regime.

(2) Abdel Moneim Aboul Fotouh (former leader of the Muslim Brotherhood; left the MB to become presidential candidate) was also one of the first candidates. He promotes himself as someone who unifies people. Despite his conservative past, he is a progressive Muslim and was an early supporter of the revolution. This is why many young revolutionaries are campaigning for him. Strangely enough, he also has the support of the Salafis, as they don't want to support the candidate of the Muslim Brotherhood. However, many Egyptians distrust Aboul Futouh as they believe 'once MB always MB'.

(3) Mohamed Morsi (president of the Freedom and Justice Party from the MB) entered very late in the race. The candidate of the MB was initially Khairat Al Shater. But when he was kicked out because of 'legal reasons'[1], Morsi came in as the reserve candidate. Morsi has no charisma, but he is backed by a formidable machine: the Muslim Brotherhood. I have seen towns change overnight from no-Morsi into all-Morsi.

(4) Ahmed Shafiq (last Prime Minister under Mubarak, an army general) had to wait a long time before getting permission to run. The parliament had voted in a law that barred former ministers of Mubarak (in the past ten years) to run for president, but the Election Committee overruled that. He is the candidate of the Army and has done a huge campaign in a short period of time. Because of the deteriorated security situation in Egypt, many people like his image of law and order.

(5) Hamdeen Sabahi (long time Nasserist and revolutionary) might become the biggest surprise of the elections. Until three weeks ago, one barely heard his name mentioned. Now half of the taxi drivers say they are going to vote for him. Of all the candidates, Sabahi most embodies the revolution and secularism at the same time.

2. It is surprising but clear that three months after their huge victory in the parliamentary elections, the Muslim Brotherhood is losing ground. Many people who voted for them now despise them. Why? First of all, there is disappointment. Egyptians voted for the MB because they were the most organised and stable factor after the revolution and thus the best guarantee to help Egypt move forward again. Egyptians were so enthusiastic about the new parliament that they watched the live broadcasts of plenary

---

1 See '9. President Morsi: cooperating or disappearing?' (25 June 2012) for more information.

sessions every day. There they saw MB not doing what they had hoped for. Secondly, Egyptians are angry about one specific promise broken: MB had said they would never issue a presidential candidate. The moment Khairat Al-Shater announced his candidacy, the reaction of many people was very harsh: MB wants all the power and we will not let this happen. A Gallup poll[2] confirms this tendency, saying that MB has lost one third of their support since February.

3. In general, this campaign has proven that the role of Islam in people's life and convictions is much more complex than assumed. One could say that Egyptians are very religious, but don't like someone to impose on them how to be religious. Moreover, the debate on how to combine Islam and democracy is far from over, and is likely never to end. A great majority of Egyptians do support article 2 of the constitution that declares Islamic law (Sharia) the main source of legislation. At the same time, they fiercely disagree on what exactly Sharia is and how to interpret it. For many, article 2 is what the 'Judeo-Christian tradition' was for the European Constitution.

4. Not one candidate likes Israel, but the fiercest opponent is not an Islamist but the socialist-Nasserist Hamdeen Sabahi. He has openly said many times that the peace treaty should be thrown in the dustbin. One should also not forget that Amr Moussa became popular as foreign minister by being tough on Israel. If we can believe a study by Brookings[3], a large majority sees Israel and the United States as the biggest threats to their country and the world in general.

Obama has lost a lot of popularity, while Erdoğan remains a hero. It is hard to say what the current perception of the EU is. But in general, people have no idea what the EU is doing in Egypt – they even don't know the EU is giving money to the country. Europe does have huge opportunities in the region, but a lot of work needs to be done.

---

2   See Gallup, 18 May 2012, Support for Islamists Declines as Egypt's Election Nears, http://www.gallup.com/poll/154706/Support-Islamists-Declines-Egypt-Election-Nears.aspx
3   Brookings Report, 21 May 2012, What Do Egyptians Want? Key Findings from the Egyptian Public Opinion Poll, http://www.brookings.edu/research/reports/2012/05/21-egyptian-election-poll-telhami

Whatever the results of this historic election, it is clear that, from today on, we can add Egypt to the list of the world's democracies. And this is thanks to all those brave revolutionaries who risked their lives, time and again, on and around Tahrir Square. As Europe failed to support the revolution, it should use this new key moment and make sure it finally acts like the neighbour Egypt deserves.

7. How to safeguard the revolution in Egypt: an outsider's perspective
Published on *EU Observer*, 26 May 2012

The following piece is the first in a row for which I used "An outsider's perspective" in the title. As explained earlier, I did this in order to be able to give political advice without making it look like foreign interference. The piece was immediately translated into Arabic and distributed around Twitter. A few days later, a friend called to say that my piece was being discussed on the program of Yosri Fouda, a respected talk show in Egypt. Fouda tried for 45 minutes to convince his guest, presidential candidate Mohamed Morsi, to agree on my five points. In the end Morsi agreed. Over the following two days Fouda did the same with Hamdeen Sabahi, the presidential candidate that came third in the first round of the presidential elections, and with liberal politician Amr Hamzawy. The fact that Morsi then did not follow the plan, became, for some, an indication that he was not trustworthy.

Two days before the presidential elections, I hosted a dinner at my place with a few revolutionaries and bloggers. One of them suddenly asked: "What are we going to do if it's a run-off between Morsi and Shafiq?" A moment of silence followed.

Nobody had really thought this a possibility. Voting for Morsi would give the Muslim Brotherhood all power in Egypt, a secular's worst nightmare. Voting for Shafiq, the former prime minister under Mubarak, would set the revolution back to square one, a revolutionary's worst nightmare.

But here we are... The worst-case scenario for the secular revolutionaries is today's reality. How could this have happened? The answer is quite obvious: fragmentation. It was fragmentation that led to the defeat of the secular forces in the parliamentary elections earlier this year, and it is fragmentation that blocked revolutionary candidates from making it to the second round of the presidential elections. If they had combined forces, they would have easily made it through. But for some reason, every revolutionary wants to become the next president of Egypt.

So what do we do now? Boycotting the run-off is useless. If you don't participate in the election, you have no right to comment afterwards.

Counting on a new revolution, assuming there has been no electoral fraud, is not right: you cannot demand democratic elections and then refuse to recognize the results if you don't like them. Not even if you profoundly dislike them. Doing nothing at all, finally, and giving everybody the freedom to vote for the candidate he dislikes least, is the worst strategy as it throws away the power of all revolutionary votes combined and leaves the revolution empty-handed.

In my opinion, there is only one way to safeguard the revolution: think strategically and negotiate! Neither Morsi nor Shafiq are sure who will win the presidency. No doubt both of them are desperate for any proposal that could lead to victory. With some 40% of the votes, the revolutionaries have a greater power and thus leverage than most might imagine. Here lies the opportunity. For once, the other candidates should stick together. As one block, they should offer their support in exchange for non-negotiable conditions. The secular/revolutionaries must be guaranteed on paper 1) the vice-president, 2) the prime minister, 3) half of the government ministries, 4) half plus one of the seats in the Constitutional Committee 5) that all decisions will be signed by both the president and the vice-president. This is politics. This is democracy.

Public statements will not safeguard the revolution, but tough negotiations can. I would first go to Morsi with this package. If he agrees, the power of the Muslim Brotherhood and the new president of Egypt will be seriously reduced. But he will realise this is the only way to unite the country again and help it move forward. If he refuses, it means that the Muslim Brotherhood and not Egypt is top of his agenda. In that case, go with the same package to Shafiq.

Is this package the ultimate guarantee that the voice of the revolution will always be heard? Perhaps not, but if one of the candidates agrees, signs the agreement and announces this publicly during the campaign, he cannot act as if it doesn't exist once he is elected. This will give the revolutionary forces the opportunity to safeguard what millions of Egyptians have been fighting for. If the next president of Egypt breaks his promises, then – and only then – a second revolution can begin.

8. Out of the crisis with an Egyptian triumvirate? An outsider's perspective
Published on *EU Observer*, 3 June 2012

This piece was written when it became clear that the first scenario (see previous piece) wouldn't fly. By this stage thousands of people were on Tahrir Square, demanding that the aims of the revolution be respected. On 2 June, the day before this was published online, Mubarak was sentenced to life in prison. To my surprise, my blog post was discussed on Tahrir Square and from the echoes of that debate on Twitter, I understood most seemed to agree with it. It was also discussed within the highest echelons of the Muslim Brotherhood. Morsi had a meeting with Hamdeen Sabahi and Abdel Moneim Aboul Fotouh about the proposal and the possibility of implementing it. One of my sources told me it was Sabahi who refused the proposal, but it is unlikely we will ever know what really transpired.

A triumvirate is a political system in which the leadership is given to three dominating political figures. In the past, it has been used in times of crisis to solve major problems and lead the state into a new era. The most well-known triumvirate of ancient times is that of Caesar in Rome[1], where it was made to balance powers and to bridge a difficult period. Also famous is the triumvirate in France by Napoleon[2] (1799–1804) in order to safeguard the French revolution.

In the current situation in Egypt, a triumvirate could be the solution. Egypt is experiencing a major crisis, and it is looking for a guarantee of civil and religious liberties and wants to safeguard the revolution. How would this triumvirate work in practice?

1. Before the elections (preferably this weekend), the main presidential candidates, Morsi, Sabahi and Aboul Fotouh, agree to form a triumvirate (or presidential three-man council) in order to face the elections of 16–17

---

1 Gaius Julius Caesar, Marcus Licinius Crassus and Gnaeus Pompeius Magnus formed a triumvirate from 60 to 53 BC, the year when Crassus died.
2 Napoleon Bonaparte formed a triumvirate, called the Consulate, with Jean Jacques Régis de Cambacérès and Charles-François Lebrun from 1799 until 1804, when Napoleon became Emperor of France.

June together. It is very important to ask for a mandate through elections. Any other option would be a major setback for democracy.

2. If they win, they agree to work together for the next four years in this triumvirate. They need enough time to be able to make the necessary changes and reforms.

3. They will be equal in hierarchy.

4. They will have clear separated competences that comprise and divide all executive powers, but decisions will be taken together.

5. The division could be as follows:
- President 1 will be responsible for the reform of everything that lies in the competences of social, economic, cultural and educational affairs. He will lead the government.
- President 2 will be responsible for the writing of the Constitution. He will lead the Constitutional Committee. He will also be responsible for the reforms of the Ministry of Interior. He will be responsible for civil and religious liberties.
- President 3 will be responsible for anything related to foreign affairs and defence, for the relationship with the military and for the reform of the judiciary system.

6. They agree to balance the composition of the government and the Constitutional Committee with all groups that exist in Egypt.

Sometimes, history can be useful for finding creative solutions. But of course, this is just an idea from an outsider's perspective.

9. President Morsi: cooperating or disappearing?
Published in Belgian weekly news magazine *Knack*, 25 June 2012

Due to the inability of the presidential candidates to make a 'revolutionary compromise' and share power, it was clear from the beginning that if president Mohamed Morsi did not cooperate with the opposition, they would automatically unify it against him. I stood on Tahrir Square when his victory was announced. I stood there again when it was announced that he was no longer Egypt's president.

Tensions ran high on Tahrir Square on Sunday 24 June 2012. Hundreds of thousands of supporters of presidential candidate Morsi gathered to hear the announcement of election results. Although all data pointed to a win for the Muslim Brothers, none were at ease. A few kilometers down the road, in Nasr City, an equally large crowd of Shafiq supporters was just as convinced of its victory. And few Muslim Brothers trusted the military.

The past week has shown the military leadership to be capable of anything, even the dissolution of parliament. On edge, the crowd at Tahrir listened to every word of the official election commission on their little mobile radios. When, after a tedious introduction and the obligatory delays, Mohamed Morsi was declared Egypt's new president, joy erupted as I have never seen before. Elderly men around me burst into tears. Strangers fell into each other's arms. Prayers were murmured and fireworks lit. It was as if the fear and frustration of decades of oppression had been compressed into the emotions of this moment.

It is, of course, a historic moment. For the first time in Egypt's history, elections have declared a non-general president.

As always with elections, celebrations are not universal. Some supporters of Ahmed Shafiq, Mubarak's last prime minister and air force general, were so distraught that they passed out on the spot. The large group of secular liberals and revolutionaries too felt little cause for jubilation.

The most common reaction expressed, however, was joy over Shafiq's loss and regret over Morsi's win. Many saw the choice between Morsi and Shafiq as one between the pest and cholera. Some had scribbled on ballots that they refused to choose between a military and a Muslim dictatorship.

Fear of the Muslim Brotherhood runs deep in many Egyptians, and not just with the Copts[1]. Word is that they can't be trusted and that they proved this over the past few months. For example, despite proclaiming to want to share power and that they would not advance a presidential candidate, they did exactly the opposite. They obtained a near majority in parliament and an actual majority in the committee that was to write the constitution and nominated Khairat Al-Shater as their presidential candidate.

These broken promises and parliament's malfunctioning cost the Muslim Brotherhood no less than 35 percent of the electorate it won compared to at parliamentary elections five months ago.

What caused these strategic errors? As with every transition from dictatorship to democracy, the people are extremely impatient. People insist that their vote immediately changes their lives. Even those that hold all power can never live up to such expectations.

The Muslim Brothers knew very well how hard a task they faced. But so did the military. Consequently the army denied them all levers for change. Without president or government, a parliamentary majority is largely impotent and left with few options. That frustration led to Khairat Al-Shater's candidacy on 31 March 2012.

The military was not pleased with this development and intervened immediately. The constitutional committee was declared unconstitutional, the Al-Shater candidacy considered inadmissible. Shortly afterwards, the Constitutional Court ruled that parliament's composition was unconstitutional too and military leadership proceeded to disband it.

On the evening of the second round of the presidential elections (16-17 June 2012), that same military leadership proclaimed legislative powers to be constitutionally theirs and that the elected president was to have no say on matters of security, information and defense. Countless false announcements of Hosni Mubarak's death succeeded in confusing those who took to the streets in protest against all this.

If there's one lesson the Muslim Brothers should have learned these past few months, it is that they won't win any of the battles they choose to fight alone. The inevitable result will be that lingering fear will shift to hatred. Limited as his options are, Morsi must realize that he will get only one shot at this. This realisation will force him to enter into a dialogue

---

[1] See '1. There is no problem with the Copts…' (12 October 2011) for some background on the Coptic Christians in Egypt.

with the military and to cooperate with secular liberals, revolutionaries and Christians in Egypt.

The choice before the Muslim Brothers is a simple one: either they try to push through their own agenda and Egypt turns on them, or they form a large coalition in the interest of all Egyptians. If they choose the former they will be wiped out in the next elections; if they choose the latter, the Muslim Brotherhood will inevitably evolve into a conservative yet democratic party.

10. Morsi is a blessing for Egyptian liberals: an outsider's perspective
Published on *EU Observer*, 26 June 2012

This is without doubt the piece for which I have been attacked most in Europe. It was meant as advice to the fragmented liberal opposition. My point was: at least all cards were on the table now the elections were over. The liberal opposition would be able to play a role only if it united and set a few clear goals. However, the liberals did not unite until the Constitutional Declaration of President Morsi in November 2012 and the constitutional referendum in December 2012, when they launched the National Salvation Front under the leadership of Mohamed El Baradei.

I was standing in the middle of Tahrir Square when Morsi was announced as the first democratically elected president in the history of Egypt. I have never seen such an outburst of happiness and relief. People cried, prayed and chanted. It felt as if, for the people on the square, 84 years of suppression and fear had finally come to an end. The liberal revolutionaries of 25 January of the previous year, however, were absent. Most of them were sitting at home, watching the result with glazed eyes. Their anxiety – that in the end the Muslim Brotherhood would take over the revolution – had become reality. They hadn't forgotten that Morsi and other leaders from the Brotherhood had initially refused to join the revolution. Morsi had even said on TV that they were talking to the regime in order to find a negotiated solution.

However, one must admit, Morsi deserves the presidency. The Muslim Brotherhood was not only the best organized, it (frankly) was also the only party with a comprehensive and coherent programme. Besides, no one can claim they didn't also suffer under the country's military rule since 1952. Furthermore, the truth is that, inside the liberal camp, the battle was about egos rather than about the future of Egypt. The fact that Hamdeen Sabahi refused to form a presidential team and negotiate with Morsi for half of the power for the secular camp in the government and the constitutional committee, is more than symbolic.

Nevertheless, the victory of Morsi is probably the best that could have happened. First of all, the only force capable of threatening the army not to leave the path towards democracy is the Muslim Brotherhood. The Supreme Council of Armed Forces (SCAF) fears them, which most probably is the reason the generals didn't dare to rig the elections (massively) or give the presidency to Shafiq. Secondly, after winning the parliamentary and presidential elections, the Muslim Brothers finally must prove to the Egyptian people that they are not only 'good Muslims', but real democrats and good rulers as well. If they can't prove this, they will be punished in the next elections. The third reason why it is good that Morsi won the presidency is that the result brings clarity. No more doubts as to whether they are to be trusted, no more conspiracy theories, no more 'what ifs'. Morsi is president and he will be held accountable only for what he does and does not realize. The debate now is about facts and no longer about rumours.

This is an opportunity for the liberal/secular/revolutionary camp. With the election of Morsi, a new era has begun: the era of politics. When there is on the one side the SCAF and on the other side the president, it is time to organise the missing part: the liberal opposition. Time has come to create the liberal alternative. The potential for this alternative is huge, as we saw in the first round of the presidential elections[1]. In order to convert this potential into an electoral victory, the following universal political laws should be taken into account:

1. Don't try to negotiate functions in the government if you're weak. Also forget about presidential teams, councils, etc. It's too late for that. Right now the only legitimate politician is Mohamed Morsi. The government is his responsibility, as are the realisations of this government. He is responsible, but also accountable for what will go wrong.
2. Stop the fragmentation. Unite forces. It is of no use to have dozens of parties with the same programme and the same aims. All the meetings with all party presidents led to nothing[2]. Small parties with less than five Members of Parliament should realise that it doesn't make sense to continue alone.

---

[1] The Islamist candidates together gained only 43,26 percent of the votes: Mohamed Morsi (24,78), Abdel Moneim Aboul Fotouh (17,41) and Mohamed Salim Al-Awa (1,01). This means that 56,74 percent of the Egyptians voted for secular candidates.
[2] There were numerous meetings in order to make alliances between parties or to join forces. No alliance really survived, until the National Salvation Front was created in November 2012.

3. Talk about content not tactics. People want to hear about solutions to their problems and not about tactical games. Don't talk only about what you don't want, but also about what your vision, your agenda is for the future of Egypt. Make a positive narrative in which solutions to the everyday problems have their proper place.
4. The duty of the opposition is to oppose. Be the watchdog of the new president and his government. Be constructive, give alternative solutions, but be harsh when necessary. Play the role of the parliament and control the executive powers. But don't criticize everything. Pick your fights.
5. Talk to the people. Explain to the streets what you want and why. And listen to what they really expect from you. Only if you can convince the people of what you're doing, can you become an alternative and win elections.

The first challenge for the liberal opposition is going to be the new constitution. The first fight will be about the procedure. If one needs a two-thirds majority, it doesn't really matter if Islamists have 49, 52 or 57 percent of the seats. The second fight will concern content. The liberal opposition should agree on five or 10 priorities or breaking points. Together they have a 'blocking minority', which is enough votes to ask for whatever they want.

Normally, Egypt will have, in the six to eight months to come, a referendum, parliamentary and presidential elections and even local elections. If the liberal parties are capable of joining forces and create a credible liberal opposition, the election of Mohamed Morsi will have been a blessing for the future of Egypt.

11. Belgium: unconstitutional parliament for 10 years and still rolling!
Published on *Beit El Hiwar*, 9 July 2012

The following piece has been used and abused ad nauseam. When President Morsi announced in July 2012 that he would be overruling the decision of the Supreme Council of Armed Forces (SCAF) to dissolve the Egyptian parliament, many considered this illegal. The SCAF had based its decision on a ruling of the Supreme Constitutional Court stating that one third of parliament had been elected in an unconstitutional manner. My point in this piece was that dissolving parliament was just one of the options available to the SCAF in response to the Court's previous ruling. That at least is the experience of this Belgian. My piece was translated into Arabic and went viral. On Facebook it was shared 19,000 times. The Muslim Brotherhood – obviously happy with my take on the matter – even made leaflets of my piece (with my picture included) and spread these in the streets of Cairo.

What the hell?! That was the reaction of most Egyptians when President Morsi announced his plans to reinstall parliament and to hold new parliamentary elections 60 days after the approval of a new constitution. Obviously this decision erases the earlier decree by the Supreme Council of Armed Forces that dissolved parliament and put down an own timetable for elections.

I must admit that Morsi surprises me. Frankly, after the many friendly, almost cozy pictures of Morsi and the generals during the transfer of power ceremony, I had thought he would avoid big political clashes between himself and the SCAF. I was wrong. Reactions in Egypt are mixed. For some, Morsi has done a heroic act because he is pushing back the army, for others he is merely trying to reinstall parliament because of its Islamist majority. We will see in the future who's right and who's wrong.

One argument, however, is hard for a Belgian to understand: some say Morsi's decision is illegal and unconstitutional. Belgians have known a very similar constitutional problem. In 2002, the Belgian coalition government decided to enlarge the electoral circumscriptions for the federal parliament. In 2003, one month before the federal elections, the Constitutional Court ruled that for one circumscription, the province of

Flemish Brabant, this electoral law was unconstitutional. The court also ruled that the problem be solved within four years.

The exact problem with the law is hard to explain. It concerns one of the complex language structures of Belgium and the fact that bilingual Brussels lies in a mostly Dutch-speaking province. I remember that moment very well, as I was one of the candidates on this unconstitutional list. In any case, it is clear that a part of the Belgian parliament after the elections of 2003 was elected in an unconstitutional way. The new government, in which I was advisor to the prime minister, tried everything to find a solution for this constitutional problem, but the coalition could not reach agreement. Unfortunately.

Therefore they decided to organise the next parliamentary elections four years minus one week after the previous elections, in 2007. The new elected parliament had the same constitutional problem, however. The new government again could not agree on a solution. That's why the 2010 elections too were held with an unconstitutional electoral circumscription. Last month, June 2012, parliament finally voted in favour of a solution. This means that only in 2014, with the next elections, will Belgium have a constitutional parliament.

During the past 10 years, this parliament has nonetheless made important decisions. In short, if the Egyptian Constitutional Court decides that one third of the Egyptian parliament has been elected unconstitutionally, many options are available as to how to deal with this problem. I am not saying Egypt should follow Belgium's approach (please, make it shorter). The Belgian example only makes clear that what Morsi did is surely political, but I wouldn't call it illegal.

12. Egypt and the psychology of dictatorship: an outsider's perspective
Published on *EU Observer*, 25 November 2012

More than anything else, the constitutional decree President Morsi signed on 22 November 2012 was the beginning of his end. I had the opportunity to talk to a few people close to the president and I was shocked by what I heard. One of them, a presidential advisor, resigned, while another has quit politics altogether. The Western world seemed to underestimate the waves this decree made in the entire Arab world[1]. It would discredit the Muslim Brotherhood in every single Arab country. Many suddenly realized that the Muslim Brotherhood was less democratic than we thought. They could have taken a very different path... The following 6 posts cover this turn of events.

What was Morsi thinking on the evening of 22 November? Everyone expected him to take measures to appease the clashes at the commemorations of the many killed revolutionaries one year ago in Mohamed Mahmud Street. Instead, he made a Constitutional Declaration of seven articles, giving himself unlimited powers.

Article 2 says: "All constitutional declarations, laws and decrees made since Morsi assumed power on 30 June 2012 cannot be appealed or canceled by any individual, or political or governmental body until a new constitution has been ratified and a new parliament has been elected. All lawsuits against them are declared void."

Article 6 says: "The president is authorized to take any measures he sees fit in order to preserve the revolution, to preserve national unity or to safeguard national security."

Not only the world was stunned. Mohamed Morsi himself was surprised by the overall negative reaction. Didn't he take these powers to give pensions to revolutionaries who were blinded[2], to reopen the trials that let those responsible for the killings be left unpunished, to give the liberals more time to finish the constitution? And above all, didn't he fire

---

1 See, for example, the consequences in Jordan: 'And revolution again in Jordan', (ALDE Report, 29 November 2012).
2 See '2. Towards a second Egyptian revolution' (20 November 2011) for details.

one of the most hated remnants of the old regime, the public prosecutor, who refused to investigate so many of the cases filed by revolutionaries?

What was Morsi thinking when he issued his declaration? Was it amateurism or bad will?

A lot of people at the commemorations on Tahrir said something to this effect: "Told you so. The Muslim Brotherhood is a Masonic-like organization who wants to take power in order to turn Egypt into a second Iran." I believe the problem lies elsewhere.

In private I asked sources close to the president and the government what was going on. Their response struck the historian in me. The story unfolded: the government had proof that the judges, the administration and the media were conspiring against the president and the government – not to overthrow them but to block whatever they wanted to do to make progress. The media, they said, did not bring the good news; they only criticized. No wonder, because they were paid by foreign funds. There was even proof that some liberals were involved in the conspiracy.

Sure, there is some truth to this. The media hasn't been very kind. The Constitutional Court dissolved the People's Assembly and is poised to dissolve the Constituent Assembly[3] as well. The public prosecutor has indeed not been very cooperative. The judges seem to have used legal grounds to motivate political rulings. The bureaucracy is dragging decisions into the administrative mud. And the liberals walked out of the Constituent Assembly. But labelling all this a conspiracy is more than one step too far. I have worked in opposition and government in Belgium. Every politician gets that feeling at least once in his career. The 'they are all against us' motive is a classic. It happens in all countries throughout the world. The question is: how do you react to it?

The biggest danger is to go into a 'bunker mentality', closing yourself up in retreat, waiting for the right moment for a counter-attack. In a fully fledged democracy, a counter-attack is always pretty harmless, because the bunker mentality makes you misread the situation and lose the next election. Former French president Nicolas Sarkozy is a good example. In a post-revolutionary situation, however, the counter-attack is for the most

---

3   The Constituent Assembly was composed by the newly elected Egyptian parliament on 26 March 2012. As 66 of the 100 members were Islamist, the non-Islamist actors boycotted the meetings. On 7 June 2012, there was an agreement to form a more balanced assembly, after it was ruled non-constitutional by the Constitutional Court. However, many members resigned in protest of Islamists dominating the constitutional protest.

part dangerous. Because whatever you decide, your bunker mentality will make you only more suspicious and will encourage you to go down the path of dictatorship, step by step.

Egypt has seen this evolution before. When Gamal Abdel Nasser took power in 1952, he didn't shut down democracy immediately. I think his initial intentions were good. He wanted to liberate Egypt from its foreign occupiers and their puppets. But then he was drawn into the bunker mentality. He didn't trust his former friends anymore and he certainly did not trust the political parties that wanted to block his plans. Gradually, Nasser turned into a brutal dictator, sacking President Naguib, abolishing political parties and imprisoning all 'anti-revolutionary forces'. This is the psychology of post-revolutionary dictatorship: fighting the enemy of the revolution from an ever-smaller bunker. Many revolutionary leaders went down the same path. After the French Revolution, some leaders wanted to fight against the counter-revolutionary forces. They weren't butchers by nature. On the contrary, they were mainly intellectuals who were suddenly overwhelmed by the fear that the revolution might fail. Lenin made the same mistake. Initially, he wanted to install a government out of representatives of the Soviets. The Soviets were the councils set up by soldiers, farmers and workers against the reign of the Tsar. But when the councils – without which no revolution would have been possible – criticized the plans of Lenin, he labelled them enemies of the people and sent them to Siberia.

I am not saying that Morsi is a dictator or that the Muslim Brothers are as ruthless as the Bolsheviks. But they should realize that there is no such thing as a 'big conspiracy' against them. There is simply no human brain with the capacity to master media, judges, politicians and the street. That only exists in James Bond films. Most people just fight for their ideas or for their own position. Of course, there are many opponents who would like to see those in power fail, but that is the case in every democracy. Central European countries needed two decades to become well-functioning democracies after the fall of the Berlin Wall. Transition is not easy and it takes an awful lot of time to achieve.

The problem is that once you go down the path to dictatorship, there is rarely a way back. So Morsi has the choice: either he sticks with his declaration and has to start a crackdown to maintain it, or he leaves his bunker, cancels his declaration and faces the difficulties every post-revolutionary transition has to deal with. There is always a way out. The president and the opposition should start a dialogue instead of setting ultimatums. Deleting articles 2 and 6 and agreeing on a way to move forward with the Constitutional Assembly might be the only solution to avoid a major political deadlock. It is not easy and often very frustrating. But thinking that a short period of dictatorship will set everything right, is wrong. History proves that the path to democracy never leads through dictatorship.

13. To safeguard democracy in Egypt, postpone the referendum: an outsider's perspective
Published on *EU Observer*, 10 December 2012

On 22 December 2012, president Morsi took a Constitutional Decree in order to push forward the new constitution. The reason for this power grab was his fear that the Constitutional Court would call the Constituent Assembly unconstitutional. With his decree he took all power and accelerated the constitutional process. On 30 November, the Constituent Assembly approved the 234 articles of the new constitution, although all non-Islamist members had resigned. This Islamist constitution needed approval by a referendum on 15 and 22 December 2012. As it was a partisan constitution, this referendum generated a storm of reaction. Eventually, the constitution was approved with 63,83 percent. However, in Cairo the constitution failed to obtain a majority of the votes.

Egypt is in total chaos. In a few days, its people will have to vote on the new constitution of the country. This is a moment of utmost importance. If Egypt votes in favour, it will set the tone for all politics in the next 10 years. Such an important decision should be made with at least some knowledge and in a calm atmosphere. Egypt's situation today is the complete opposite.

The chaos started with President Morsi's Constitutional Declaration[1] on 22 November. In this decree, he took all power to prevent the Supreme Constitutional Court from aborting the constitutional process. This would have been a logical step for the Court as it had declared the People's Assembly unconstitutional before – and it was this assembly that selected the Constitutional Assembly. Morsi believed that the court was taking a political, rather than a legal, point of view, with one goal: to obstruct the Islamist majority. True or not, Morsi went further than necessary for his purpose.

When the Islamist majority (the others had left) approved the constitution in a rush, everything pointed in the direction of an Islamist

---

1   See '12. Egypt and the psychology of dictatorship: an outsider's perspective', 25 November 2012.

takeover of the country. Most worrying indeed, but the question is whether it is illegitimate? I think everyone agrees that Morsi's power grab was not legitimate. I am sure he thinks so himself. More important, however, is whether the constitution is illegitimate. Frankly, I don't see why it would be. The people elected the People's Assembly. Following the constitution, one third of all the candidates should have been independent from any party. But they weren't independent at all. However, not only the Freedom and Justice Party failed to do that; all parties were complicit. So the People's Assembly might be unconstitutional, but it is not undemocratic or illegitimate. (By the way, I have never understood why nobody mentioned to all parties before the elections that MPs would be barred from running for these seats.) In any case, this freely and fairly elected assembly selected a Constitutional Assembly of 100 people. One can discuss whether this selection is fair, but it is certainly not undemocratic or illegitimate.

Why did so many representatives run out of the Constitutional Assembly? Writing a constitution is not the same as drawing up a budget. The latter can easily be approved by a majority against opposition. That's politics. But a constitution is different. Constitutions are essentially the protection of minorities, of weaker groups and people, of individual freedom as well. Constitutions offer protection of minorities against the majority. The fact that several 'minorities' felt insufficiently heard gives this constitution an element of fundamental unfairness. But that doesn't make it illegitimate.

In short, President Morsi took power in an illegitimate way to protect a legitimate draft constitution. But that doesn't mean that the constitution is a fair and fully democratic piece. Also, from a legal point of view, one might have some questions. For example, how on earth can a constitution say that it is forbidden to insult a human being? Is telling my neighbour that I don't like his shirt unconstitutional?

But back to the chaos… The drama of the last days is of almost mythical proportions. As of today, it is totally unclear what the opposition's position is. They said yesterday that they are against all presidential decrees. But, at the same time, some of them are campaigning for a 'no' in the referendum. It is also unclear if the opposition (or a part of it) will boycott the referendum. Some say Morsi has to go, others that he has to change his decrees and change the constitution.

The chaos at the president's side, however, is even more baffling. The day after he gave his (much delayed) speech in which he stated that nothing is going to change in the constitution, vice president Mekki said some things might change. To confuse matters further, Mekki said the President might delay the referendum, while presidential advisor, Al-Awa said that a delay is impossible. The President said the constitution is not going to change, but shortly after he stated (through his spokesman) that if the opposition agrees on the articles in the constitution it doesn't like, he will put these articles in a separate law and bring it to the next parliament. One week before the referendum the President issued a law that increases taxes on a lot of things, but he cancels the law the same night at 2.30 am. The government wasn't informed. And there is also the question of the organisation of the referendum. Some judges decided to boycott, others said they will overview. What is the army going to do? Who is going to count the votes? Who is going to supervise the counting of the votes?

This is the atmosphere in which the people of Egypt have to decide on the most important document of the next 10 years, at least. One can disagree on whether the constitution or the process is democratic or not. But one cannot but agree that a referendum in the current state would be undemocratic. Democracy is essentially a system that allows us to disagree in a civilized way. It also means giving people a chance to disagree. Organizing the referendum in one week's time is denying the people the chance to discuss the constitution and, yes, also to disagree.

So there are essentially two sides. Morsi and his Islamist forces are confident that this constitution is fair and representative of Egypt's values. And they are confident of victory. Fine. Then they should have no problem with a delay. The other side feels the constitution is flawed and does not represent Egypt's values. Fine again. Then they too should support only one constitutional decree: one that allows a 30-day delay to properly make their case to the Egyptian voters. So it becomes simple: hold the referendum in mid-January 2013. And let's have a proper debate.

14. The suicide mission of the Muslim Brotherhood: an outsider's perspective
Published on *EU Observer*, 12 April 2013

After the constitutional declaration and the referendum, Egypt was deeply polarized. It was an Islamist document, written by Muslim Brothers and Salafis. It also triggered the formation of the National Salvation Front, an alliance of all the other political forces. The leader of the Front became Nobel Prize winner Mohamed El Baradei. Many people feared that what president Morsi did, was only the beginning of an Islamist project. It was the start of what would end with the huge protests of 30 June 2013 and the army deposing the president.

When Mohamed Morsi was elected as the first civilian president of Egypt in June 2012, most reform-minded people were hopeful. Like many leaders of the Muslim Brotherhood, Morsi spent many years in prison. No doubt they would do everything to change this 'society of paranoia', right? In his first speech as elected president, Morsi promised to form an inclusive government and to appoint a female and a Coptic vice-president. The main question back in June was how Morsi would deal with the army: in a 'mini-coup', they had curtailed the president's position and dissolved the People's Assembly[1].

And yes, Morsi's first decisions were bold. He tried to reinstall the People's Assembly. He turned back the mini-coup and took back power. On top of this, he fired Field Marshall Tantawi, the head of the army and the SCAF (and his number two, Sami Anan) and replaced him with General Sisi, the head of the Military Intelligence of Egypt. Morsi also appointed as his presidential advisors people from all over the political and religious spectrum. All these steps were of major importance. Not only for Egypt, which seemed to be on the way towards rapid reform from autocratic to democratic state... The entire world was watching closely.

Moreover, one should not underestimate the leading role Egypt plays in the Arab world. Egypt is by far the most populated country and claims the

---

[1] See '13. To safeguard democracy in Egypt, postpone the referendum: an outsider's perspective', 10 December 2012

historical leadership of the Arab society. No less important is the fact that the largest political organisation in the Arab world has its origins and its leadership in Egypt: the Muslim Brotherhood. The Muslim Brotherhood in Egypt is like the Communist Party in Russia during the Soviet-Union. All sister parties in the region are closely following what they say and do.

Generous in victory, gracious in defeat?

Contrary to their promises, the Muslim Brotherhood was not very generous in victory. No female or Coptic vice-president was appointed. The government appeared not to be inclusive. The presidential advisors from outside the Brotherhood were not listened to, while those of the Brotherhood had nothing to say. Very soon, the old underground culture of following orders instead of discussing them found its place at the presidential palace. Suspicion returned too: *everyone is against us*. The consequence was a bunker mentality[2]: outside the bunker, there is a huge conspiracy against the Muslim Brotherhood. The only option is to fight back.

So, that's what the Muslim Brotherhood did, fight back. First they replaced the editors in chief of most of the main newspapers. Then they tried to sideline liberal and Coptic voices in the Constitutional Committee. Then Morsi took all power by presidential decree. He sidelined the Constitutional Court and installed his own public prosecutor[3]. He finished the Constitution and put it to a referendum two weeks later.

As the reaction of the people was much bigger than they had expected, the Muslim Brothers saw their conspiracy theory confirmed. The only solution was to fight back even harder. On the streets and through the courts. The new public prosecutor started accusing opposition politicians, activists and random people in the street.

However, it must be said that the opposition wasn't gracious in defeat either. After they organized themselves in the National Salvation Front (NSF), they boycotted pretty much everything. By doing so, the NSF didn't miss an opportunity to miss an opportunity. They refused to talk to

---

2   See '12. Egypt and the psychology of dictatorship: an outsider's perspective' (25 November 2012) for a discussion of the emergence and perils of a 'bunker mentality'.
3   The public prosecutor acts as public attorney before criminal courts, with the right to file criminal actions. This right of initiative makes the function highly political and often hated.

President Morsi, to Vice-president Mekki and to the Muslim Brotherhood. They boycotted the Constitutional Committee, the referendum and the elections. If 38 percent of Egyptians went to vote against the referendum, it was despite, and not thanks to, the opposition.

Collapse is nigh ...

If all this political turmoil were to happen in an economically prosperous environment, then citizens would react with increasing apathy. Unfortunately, the contrary is happening. Morsi launched his presidential decree[4] and the constitution during the negotiations with the IMF. Although the IMF is politically neutral, turmoil and fights in the street does make them doubt Egypt's political stability and thus ability to reform.

Today, the IMF doubts have proven correct. No deal has been made. This means that Egypt misses out on a loan of $14,5 billion in total, as the loans of institutions like the European Union, the European Bank for Reconstruction and Development and the African Union are connected to that of the IMF. At the same time the Egyptian pound is faltering, power cuts have become a daily issue, queues of cars and trucks waiting for diesel are growing. Tourism – the country's main source of income – is a disaster. Investors are waiting, while large foreign companies are, one after the other, leaving the country.

For the average Egyptian, the cost of living is becoming a nightmare. The anger is clearly growing. And instead of seeing politicians working hard to improve this situation, people see them fighting and taking decisions about blocking porn on the internet or allowing police officers to grow a beard. Instead of creating an investment-friendly environment, the Muslim Brothers are targeting activists, journalists and comedians for insulting the president or insulting religion.

The question is not if but when the situation will explode.

It is hard to overestimate the anger and the fear of the Egyptian people. You could compare it with a room full of gas. It needs only one spark to explode. That spark could well be the high subsidies for bread and energy that need to be reformed. The last time Egypt tried to cut subsidies was in 1977, under president Anwar Sadat; this immediately lead to the

---

4   See 12. Egypt and the psychology of dictatorship: an outsider's perspective' (25 November 2012).

only uncontrollable riots ever under military rule. Looking at the anarchy today in cities like Port Said, Suez or Malhalla, it is clear that no party will be able to control the streets if the situation explodes.

In the meantime, President Morsi and his government are making one mistake after the other. It's as if the Muslim Brotherhood is on a suicide mission. Not only for Egypt but also for the entire Arab world. The same day Morsi issued his decree in November 2012, the protest for political reform in Jordan was halted, as protesters feared only the Jordanian Muslim Brothers would profit. A few days ago, the Syrian Muslim Brothers even complained that their Egyptian counterparts were ruining their reputation.

We know from history that the situation in Egypt is not exceptional. France, for example, took 80 years from revolution to a stable democracy. And the transition in Central Europe took almost two decades. History teaches us that the biggest danger in times of collapse and anarchy is the rise of a new populist or strongman, someone like the Salafist Hazem Abu Ismael or a return of the army to power. That would bring the Muslim Brotherhood, as well as the opposition, back to square one.

But that doesn't mean chaos is the only way. It isn't too late to move this country forward. Egypt has everything: natural resources, a young, ambitious population and the most attractive tourism combination in the world. All that is required is for parties and politicians to forget their egos and their honour and start a real dialogue about solving problems together. The last window of opportunity is closing rapidly. Dear politicians, for the sake of the people of Egypt, don't miss this last chance. Otherwise, there will be *no* winners left.

15. And now, the end is near for President Morsi
Published on *EU Observer*, 3 July 2013

On the evening of the day this piece was published, Morsi was deposed in a live TV statement by General Sisi (Commander-in-Chief of the Egyptian Army), Mohamed El Baradei (leader of the liberal opposition), the Grand Imam of Al Azhar and the Pope of the Coptic Christians.

"We are not leaving until Morsi does." This was what I heard just about everywhere in Cairo over the past few days. Their determination was reinforced by the historic turnout on 30 June, when enormous masses took the street. The armed forces initially spoke of 13 million people, the ministry of information called it 17 million. Some media stated that, in the whole of Egypt, no less than 30 million people had taken to the streets.

Whatever the number, millions of Egyptians were united in a single message: *erhal* (leave).

Non-Egyptians wonder what Morsi must have done to get that many people into the streets. Some point to the economy as the main reason. It is true that Egypt is at the brink of an economic abyss. Every day, there are multiple outages of power and running water. There is hardly any petrol left, creating long queues at gas stations, which in turn cause big traffic jams. Tourism, Egypt's major source of income, has fallen drastically, to a fraction of what it once was[1]. The currency has lost a quarter of its value, making everything more expensive. This is particularly hard on the large group of very poor Egyptians.

Yet, this is not the reason for the massive turnout at protests. It is clearly not a hunger revolution either. While having a cup of tea close to the presidential palace, I observed the massive crowds passing by. The diversity was apparent: young and old, veiled and unveiled women, poor and rich, Muslim and Christian. Furthermore, it is important to stress that the atmosphere was, and still is, positive. Yesterday, Tahrir and its

---

[1] Egypt's tourism revenue was $5,9 billion in 2013. In 2010 the revenue was $12,5 billion. In 2010 one dollar was worth 5,8 Egyptian pound, in June 2013 it was 7 Egyptian pounds. The average inflation in 2013 was 10 percent.

neighbouring streets looked like one big festival. Fireworks were lit. There was singing and dancing.

What brings all of these people together is a sense of betrayal. The Muslim Brotherhood was given a chance after the revolution. They were the best organised and had the most thought-through ideas. People imagined the Brotherhood to be the best shot at fulfilling the ideals of the revolution: freedom, dignity, justice and bread. This is exactly what was expected of Morsi. And he had gotten off to a good start. He replaced the hated military leader Tantawi and re-seized the power the armed forces had taken from the presidency

All changed in November 2012. Morsi and his party were convinced of a major conspiracy in the making[2]. His response was a constitutional declaration seizing all power and shoving an Islamic constitution down the throats of the Egyptians. As of that moment, more and more Egyptians became convinced that Morsi was just a Muslim Brotherhood president and not the president of the Egyptian people.

That is at the core of this week's protests: people do not accept one group forcing its agenda upon an entire nation, regardless of whether that group has an electoral majority. This rising against 'the tyranny of the majority' is what we see in Egypt today, and saw in Turkey over the past few weeks. In Turkey, people do not accept the economic progress under Erdoğan's rule as an excuse to govern as he pleases.

This is Morsi's and the Muslim Brotherhood's big error of judgement: convinced of their majority, they thought the opposition was small and divided and that people would eventually side with them. 30 June revealed a very different outcome. No one can withstand such masses. Not even the army. The military brass saw what happened and saw that it could result in a huge spiral of violence. This is probably why they issued an ultimatum, to avoid Egypt turning into one giant street fight.

In the meantime, everybody is abandoning ship. Ministers have resigned. The president's press secretary has quit, as have a number of governors. Morsi and the Muslim Brotherhood are increasingly isolated as the people seem determined to continue to protest. Some claim an elected president cannot simply be deposed. That would be unusual, certainly, but not unique. US president Nixon resigned to avoid impeachment. French president Charles De Gaulle resigned upon losing a referendum.

---

2 See '14. The suicide mission of the Muslim Brotherhood: an outsider's perspective' (12 April 2013)

A referendum that was organised in response to the many street protests seen by France in those days.

Whatever the outcome of this battle of titans, some conclusions are already clear. For one thing, a religious country such as Egypt does not accept its religion being abused in power plays. Islam, like Christianity, is a diverse religion. Imposing one interpretation on the rest of the population is not tolerated. Secondly, citizens of a country in transition are aware that democracy is not just about holding elections. Whoever is elected will have to listen to all groups of society. Majority reasoning is refuted. Finally, it is clear people will not accept their hard-won freedom being restricted again, by anyone. Those who try will be removed immediately. Those are the signals in the Egyptian streets today. And those are the reasons to be optimistic about the outcome of the Arab Spring.

16. Egypt: will there be order after the chaos? An outsider's perspective
Published on *EU Observer*, 10 July 2013

The atmosphere in Egypt was ecstatic after the deposal of president Morsi, at least on the side of the ones that pushed for it. In the streets of Cairo, you could feel new hope that Egypt would move forward again. The news of the massacre of 51 Muslim Brothers in a few hours in Cairo was the first of a series of events that would disturb this feeling and turn hope into fear.

Everyone in Egypt woke up on Monday 8 July with the horrible news that the army had shot dead 51 Muslim Brothers near the barracks of the Republican Guards in Cairo. Immediately, two different stories were propagated. Muslim Brothers claimed their people were unarmed, holding a peaceful protest when suddenly the military opened fire. They showed images purporting infant casualties. The armed forces – and its sympathizers – showed images of (what appeared to be) armed Muslim Brothers trying to attack the barracks. They claim the first casualty was a soldier. They also demonstrated that the images of dead children were old footage.

This is characteristic of the propaganda battle currently raging in Egypt. This battle over truth is extremely important. It sets the mood of the international community just as much as it does that of the Egyptians. A similar propaganda battle is fought over what actually happened on Wednesday 3 July[1]: a military coup or a military intervention? This is no innocent word game but a crucial point that determines the future of Egypt and many Arab states.

To understand what is happening now, every detail of these past months is important. A brief overview: In August it was President Morsi who deposed the hated military leader Tantawi and replaced him with General Sisi. Morsi was convinced Sisi would never be disloyal. Egyptians first took to the streets in November, when Morsi grabbed all power while forcing a constitution on them. Back then, it was Sisi that called for

---
1   See '15. And now, the end is near for President Morsi' (3 July 2013)

dialogue. In the months that followed, Sisi repeatedly implored Morsi to transform his government into a coalition of national unity. Morsi refused.

When it became clear protests that were being organized for 30 June would be massive, it was again the army, by way of Sisi, who asked Morsi to present a solution. When Morsi did exactly the opposite in a speech a couple of days prior to 30 June, even threatening the opposition and saying he would sacrifice his blood if necessary, Sisi advised the president to resign in order to avoid spiraling violence. Morsi repeated that he was legitimately elected and that nothing could ever change that. For the Muslim Brothers, the prevailing sentiment was that all would eventually pass.

The number of people that turned out on 30 June was surprisingly high. Google Earth counted 33 million, which would mean more than a third of the Egyptian population. Everybody in Egypt realised that the situation would soon become untenable. Nonetheless, acting as a go-between, General Sisi sought a solution. He gave all Egyptian politicians 48 hours to come to an understanding on how to move forward. Privately, he was thinking of organizing a referendum on the presidency.

He ran that idea by the powers that be: the Islamic university Al Azhar; the Coptic church; the opposition (through Mohamed El Baradei) and by the youth that were at the origin of the so-called 'rebel campaign' (Tamarod), the organisers of the street protests. It was the youth that refused. They wanted Morsi's resignation and nothing else. One of their leaders told Sisi: "I want to tell you, sir, you might be the commander of the army, but for the moment the people are your commander. Now you must listen to the people and support us."[2] Apparently, this was the decisive contribution that led to the military's intervention. The so-called transition plan advanced by the army was a copy-and-paste transcription of the plan the 'rebel youth' had circulated earlier.

Coup or no coup, today, Egypt has two presidents: one elected president supported by the Muslim Brothers and one appointed president supported by a large majority of the Egyptian people. No side wants to budge. This is the reason for the current violence in the streets, including the military's unacceptable violence directed at pro-Morsi protesters.

What now? Either we enter a French Revolution scenario, with one faction reckoning with and seceding from another each year, finally ending

---

2   *The Huffington Post*, 8 July 2013, http://www.huffingtonpost.com/2013/07/08/mahmoud-badr-tamarod-protest-leader-egypt_n_3559487.html

in dictatorship, or genuine talks recognising and involving all political groups. Recent events clearly forfeit any scenario that includes Mohamed Morsi. What happened this week also makes it increasingly obvious that a stable future is just as impossible with the military in the cockpit. The fact that almost none of the parties and factions of the new coalition agreed on the new constitutional declaration, proposed by the army to replace the constitution, shows that the army can't just do whatever they want.

The only valid script that can bring Egypt from chaos to order will have to be based on the very principles that got 33 million Egyptians in the streets. It'll have to be an Egypt that allows everybody the freedom to be themselves. Whether they are Salafi, Muslim, Copt or even atheist. Every government or president that tries to curtail this freedom in one way or another will once again face a full Tahrir and a new revolution.

17. How President Morsi ousted himself: a too short overview

Published on *EU Observer*, 25 July 2013

This is a recap of what happened during the year of Morsi's presidency. It tries to connect all the elements that finally led to the fall of Morsi.

Confusion all around in Egypt today. Everywhere, discussions rage about whether or not the military performed a coup, if 30 June was a second revolution or a protraction of the 2011 revolution. What should one do with the Muslim Brotherhood, let alone President Mohamed Morsi, who has been kept hidden somewhere for over two weeks? My cab driver declared that he had gone to a pro-Morsi protest although he absolutely did not want the Muslim Brotherhood or Morsi to reassume power. Confusing.

However, the deep feelings of hatred that are surfacing these days are more cause for concern than the confusion. Many hate the Muslim Brotherhood and are willing to do anything to break the backbone of the organization. They're convinced the Muslim Brothers are religious totalitarians. Others hate the military, the police and all things linked to the old regime, as manifestations of all that went so very wrong in Egypt over the past decades. As for the MB, they hate everything that remotely smells like secularism. According to them, 30 June and all that preceded it, was one big conspiracy.

Actually, all are right in a way.

Who are the Muslim Brothers?

The MB was founded in 1928 by a young Egyptian teacher, Hassan Al Banna. It is no coincidence that this came just a few years after Mustafa Kemal Atatürk had abolished the Caliphate. Al Banna was convinced that Egyptians were westernizing too much and that they had to become real Muslims again. He wanted to achieve his goal by two means: resistance to the British occupation of Egypt and, above all, education of the Egyptians themselves. For all intents and purposes, Al Banna was a kind of missionary. He travelled all over Egypt, persuading as many Egyptians as possible to join his underground resistance movement.

The MB combined religious education and social aid to the poorest. It made them immensely popular in no time. Egyptian and British authorities were less enthusiastic. They saw the MB as a subversive movement and quickly took action to suppress it. The Brothers became violent and murdered the Egyptian prime minister in the forties. A year later Hassan Al Banna himself was murdered.

The average Egyptian never completely trusted the MB and this for three reasons... First, there is the ambiguity regarding their ultimate objective. Do they aim to restore the Caliphate? Do they aspire to worldwide domination? Do they seek to transform Egypt into some sort of Saudi Arabia? The second reason is congruent with the first: it being a secret organization. As with freemasons, there's no public list of members and nobody knows the organization's exact numbers. And although they deny it, the MB is organized on an international level. The secrecy has a lot to do with persecution, but also gives way to all kinds of conspiracy theories.

The third reason for mistrust is the fact that the MB used a lot of violence. Their most infamous act was the assassination of President Anwar Sadat. Despite the fact that they have since disavowed violence, many are convinced that the Brothers still are behind terrorist organizations such as Gamaa Al Islamiya or Al Qaeda. Al Zawahiri, Osama Bin Laden's successor, has an MB past[1]. It is no coincidence that every Egyptian president was on a tense footing with the Brotherhood while simultaneously being forced to deal with them.

The 2011 revolution

When, on 25 January, the first mass protests filled Tahrir, MB executives declared that its members would not join. They chose evolution, not revolution. Nonetheless, many of their young members joined the

---

[1] Ayman Al Zawahiri (Cairo, 1951) became member of the Muslim Brotherhood at the age of 14. He was the last leader or 'emir' of Islamic Jihad (Gamaa Al Islamiya), a terrorist group responsible for the murder on Egypt's president Sadat in 1981. In 1998 Zawahiri merged Islamic Jihad into Al Qaeda. He was the number 2 of Al Qaeda until Osama Bin Laden was killed in 2011. On 2 May 2011 Zawahiri became the leader of Al Qaeda.

revolutionaries at Tahrir. On 28 January, the MB realized that remaining on the sidelines was no longer an option and backed the revolution. This was important because if the organization is capable of one thing, it is raising huge crowds. That became apparent after Hosni Mubarak had fallen and the military leaders made some major errors[2]. If Tahrir needed to be filled, the Brothers delivered. It gave them a reputation of being good organizers that could speak for a large part of Egyptian society.

After all, the MB had the aura of the revolution and of decades of resistance to the dictatorship. Mohamed Morsi was pretty used to being in jail and he and many other leaders of the MB still were imprisoned on 25 January. They also enjoyed the image of being 'good Muslims' and therefore honest people, as opposed to the corrupt regime. A third advantage they held over other opposition forces: they had a plan, the so-called 'Ennahda' or Renaissance that should give Egypt its revival on all fronts.

The 2011 elections

It was no surprise the MB won the November elections in such a convincing way, with nearly 50% of the votes. The other contenders were divided, badly organized and made campaign mistakes. On the subway, someone told me plainly why he voted MB: "To marry I must buy an apartment. I can't do that if I lose my job. The economy must reboot. The MB is our best guarantee of that."

The enthusiasm in Egypt before, during and after the elections was enormous. People queued for hours to cast their true first vote. Politics, and the meaning of the newly won liberty, was discussed all over: the subway, the market, at the barber shop. After the elections, huge numbers of Egyptians listened in on parliamentary sessions broadcasted on radio. They did so in cabs, in the street, in tea houses. Every word was heard. That initiated the first step towards the MB's downfall.

Every Egyptian heard how chaotic the parliamentary debates were. They heard elected MB and Salafis table the most insane propositions. There was the representative that proposed to make it legal to have sexual intercourse with a spouse up until six hours after she died. It infuriated the

---

2   See '1. There is no problem with the Copts…' (12 October 2011) and '2. Towards a second Egyptian revolution' (20 November 2011)

average Egyptian. They had voted for the MB to improve the economy, not to discuss Islam. Popular support for the MB sank rapidly.

The 2012 presidential elections

I was sitting down with a few young revolutionaries the evening before the first round of presidential elections, when [as you may recall] one of them suddenly questioned: "What are we going to do if it's a run-off between Morsi and Ahmed Shafiq?"

That, off course, would be every revolutionary's worst nightmare[3]. Voting for Shafiq was totally out of the question. He was Mubarak's last prime minister. If he were to become president, the revolution would have been in vain. To the astonishment of many Egyptians, that nightmare choice became reality.

Although Morsi, and thus the MB, only got 25 percent in the first round (half the result of the parliamentary elections six months earlier), he got the most votes of any candidate. Seventy-five percent didn't vote MB, but that vote was divided. This was (and still is) the reality of the opposition: divided and lacking a common strategy. Yours truly suggested the revolutionary candidates endorse Morsi in return for half the power and a veto right[4]. There was never an actual deal along those lines for lack of unity in the revolutionary camp.

Muhamed Morsi had, however, accepted the proposal live on the most important talk show on TV. He had promised to be the guardian of the revolution and the president of all Egyptians and to share power with the liberal opposition. He had further promised to appoint a Coptic vice-president and a woman. What were the options available to the revolutionary voter? Let Shafiq win or reluctantly vote for Morsi, hoping his promises were not hollow.

---

3   See '7. How to safeguard the revolution in Egypt: an outsider's perspective' (26 May 2012) for a more in-depth analysis.
4   For the original proposal, see '7. How to safeguard the revolution in Egypt: an outsider's perspective' (26 May 2012)

Morsi's broken promises

I stood in the middle of Tahrir amidst a Muslim Brotherhood crowd when Muhamed Morsi was declared winner of the presidential elections and thus the first democratically elected president in the history of Egypt. The relief among those present was indescribable. It felt as if 85 years of persecution was lifted off the Brothers' shoulders. It was the week I published a piece stating that Morsi had a choice between cooperating and disappearing[5]. And that if MB failed to live up to their promises, the Egyptians' fear of them would quickly turn to hatred. That is exactly what has happened in the past year.

Still, Morsi did get off to a good start. He deposed the intensely disliked Tantawi as leader of the military and replaced him with the younger General Abdel-Fattah Al-Sisi. Tantawi had been the face of the Supreme Council of Armed Forces (SCAF) that held all power in the days between Mubarak and Morsi. It was the same SCAF that had deprived the president of power during the presidential election weekend by virtue of a hastily drawn up constitutional declaration. Having taken back that power in August, Morsi was cheered on by many Egyptians. He had an approval rating of 80%.

Other promises proved harder to realize. In his campaign, Morsi had promised to solve Cairo's traffic problems in 100 days and clean up the city. Of course, 100 days having come and gone, there was not one traffic jam or pile of rubbish less in one of the world's most chaotic cities. His promise of a woman and a Copt vice president wasn't fulfilled either, although he did appoint a widely appreciated judge.

The beginning of the end: the mini-coup

None of these shortcomings, however, were the reason for the sudden shift in atmosphere in Egypt. To everyone's surprise, in November 2012, Morsi – by way of his spokesman – issued a new constitutional declaration stripping constitutional court judges of all power. He appointed a new general prosecutor. He further declared that the drafting of the constitutions was to be concluded within the week and would be followed

---

5   See '9. President Morsi: cooperating or disappearing?' (25 June 2012)

by a referendum in the following two weeks (on a text written almost exclusively by Islamists).

Revolutionary and liberal Egypt were infuriated. Instead of being included in the political process, they had been pushed aside, together with the entire judicial power. Again, masses took to the street, protesting 'the MB coup'. The MB resorted to armed mobs to disperse the protesters. Some got dragged into the presidential palace, where they were beaten and tortured. Revolutionaries of the first hour declared Morsi to be the new Mubarak. The vice president resigned in protest, as did all independent presidential advisors.

The day after the so-called mini-coup, I asked someone close to Morsi what was going on and was told an incredible story. Morsi and the MB leadership were convinced of a major conspiracy[6] being orchestrated by opposition figures like Mohamed El Baradei, the media, judges, businessmen and elements of the old regime. Morsi and his brothers had become entrenched in a bunker mentality – of 'us against everyone else' – and they still haven't managed to let go. This induced Morsi to commit mistake after mistake. Dialogue had become impossible.

The tyranny of the majority

There were several attempts to restore dialogue. The first was made by the new Army commander, General Sisi, during the protests against the mini-coup. Morsi refused Sisi's invitation to sit around the table with the opposition. Instead, he organized his own dialogue between his advisors, the resigning vice-president and the opposition. By that time, the opposition had lost all faith. And it has to be said: the opposition was also divided to the extent that any strategy beyond boycott seemed impossible.

Despite the division, the opposition managed to organize itself into the National Salvation Front, headed by Baradei. Once the interlocutors had become clear, the European Union endeavoured to secure a kind of compromise involving power sharing between the MB and the opposition. The recommendations included: Morsi should replace his prime minister and allow the opposition access to five cabinet positions; the electoral law should be adapted according to the remarks made by

---

6 See '12. Egypt and the psychology of dictatorship: an outsider's perspective' (25 November 2012)

the Supreme Constitutional Court; and Hisham Barakat the despised general prosecutor[7], should be replaced. The European diplomacy chief, Catherine Ashton, herself came to Cairo to give this proposal a final push. All seemed to agree. But Morsi did not respond. The political leadership of the MB was divided...

Instead of trying to close the gap, a campaign was launched against leading political and media figures. Journalists were detained. Liberal politicians were accused of spying, of heresy, of conspiring. Even popular satirist Bassem Youssef was prosecuted and questioned. Morsi's approval ratings fell from 80 to 30 percent in less than seven months. More and more people saw him as the president of the Muslim Brothers, rather than as the president of all Egyptians. Those that had voted for him felt cheated. In the presidential elections they had overcome their deep doubts and anxieties in the name of the revolution. Now they felt betrayed by Morsi.

The youth rises against Morsi

On top of all the political mistakes, Egypt was doing worse economically. There were daily power and water cuts. Petrol shortages became a general occurrence, causing enormous traffic jams at every filling station. The cost of living got a lot more expensive as Egypt's pound fell. If it hadn't been for financial aid from Qatar and Libya, Egypt would probably have gone bankrupt by January 2013.

In April, some youth had the idea of starting a petition demanding precipitated presidential elections. A big demonstration was planned for 30 June, the first anniversary of Morsi's oath of office. Much to even their surprise, the response to the petition was overwhelming. Pretty soon they had gathered two million signatures. The military realized: 30 June was going to be huge and dangerous. The hatred ran deep. The Army decided to contact the founders of the rebel movement (Egyptian Tamarod Movement) and offered to provide security on condition of a peaceful demonstration.

---

7   Hisham Barakat was the public prosecutor who asked the courts to investigate famous TV satirist Bassem Youssef and well known activists like Alaa Abdel Fatah. He was also preparing cases against opposition leaders like Mohamed El Baradei.

Meanwhile, the petition amassed a spectacular number of signatures (it is said that by the end there were 22 million), leading everyone to realize this would end in an enormous clash between those who saw Morsi as a new dictator (betraying all ideals of the revolution) and the MB, who insisted on respect for the election outcome. The days leading up to 30 June already saw some skirmishes and casualties.

The role of the Egyptian Army

As an institute, the army is highly respected in Egypt, particularly because, as other institutions failed, the military often appeared to be the only group that could get things done. Even as it holds a large chunk of the country's economy (figures vary from 20 to 40 percent GDP), it is considered the only factor to put the country's interests first. During the 2011 revolution, the army chose not to intervene, which meant choosing the side of the protesters on Tahrir. In the end, it was the military that deposed Mubarak.

Of course, Morsi too saw 30 June approaching. But instead of searching for a solution, he began looking for ways to divert the people's attention and try to gather them behind him. All of a sudden, there was the problem of the Nile dam in Ethiopia and the threat of war[8]. The sentencing of NGO employees[9] drew anger in Europe and the US. And suddenly, in front of a packed soccer stadium, Morsi changed his Syria strategy and called for a jihad against Syrian president and dictator Bashar Al Assad. At the same time, Morsi refused to take tough measures to tackle the anarchy and violence in Sinai, where several soldiers had been kidnapped.

Thus, in June, the army saw the convergence of two phenomena: on the one hand, a clash between Morsi opposers and supporters with the potential to grow into a civil war; on the other hand, a president willing to risk national security for political reasons. Add to this the economic

---

8 President Morsi organized a meeting with politicians from all sides to discuss how to react against the plans of Ethiopia to build a dam on the Nile. The politicians that were present didn't know the meeting was broadcast live on television. Some proposed to start a war against Ethiopia, others to send spies to support the opposition.

9 On 4 June 2013, 43 NGO employees were sentenced to 2 to 3 years in jail for working in Egypt without a proper status and for being funded illegally. It was a clear political trial. One of my good friends, Robert Becker, was sentenced to 3 years in jail. He was the only foreigner that stayed in Egypt for the trial. He fled Egypt after the decision of the Court was taken.

consequences of all of this for a country already on the brink. General Sisi made multiple attempts to persuade Morsi to engage in dialogue with the opposition. Morsi not only refused to listen, but the political office of the MB also decided in secret to replace Sisi and a number of other generals during summer. A similar fate was bestowed upon a bunch of 'conspiring' judges and journalists.

The finale: 30 June until 3 July

The tension on the eve of 30 June was tangible. Everybody believed a massive and violent clash would ensue. Friends told me they were prepared to die – or, at least, they were convinced that this would be their fate. But when I went from Tahrir to the presidential palace and back on 30 June, I realized it was all over for Morsi. Never before had so many people taken to the streets. (Numbers vary from 15 to 33 million Egyptians.) Whatever the figure, it was clear to all that this was far bigger than the 2011 revolution itself. The protests were too big to fail.

The question then was: what would the military do? Would it wait until the situation escalated into violence before intervening or would it try to act preventively? General Sisi chose the latter. He gave Egyptian politicians (read: Morsi) 48 hours to come to a solution. Morsi rejected the ultimatum and gave a speech repeating allegations of conspiracies and foreign interference. The only 'concession' he made was the promise to hold parliamentary elections within six months.

The army intervened, backed by the liberal opposition, the Coptic pope and the head of Al Azhar, the most renowned institute of Sunni Islam. They advanced a transition plan that was verbatim the one the rebel movement had proposed two weeks earlier. I was in Tahrir Square when it was announced that Morsi had been removed from office and replaced by the presiding judge of the Constitutional Court. The mood was ecstatic. Millions of Egyptians partied, danced and sang in the streets all night long.

Revolution or military coup?

Apart from the MB themselves, few Egyptians consider the removal of Morsi a real military coup. Rather, it is regarded as a second revolution in which the military sided with the people, as was the case in the first revolution. Contrary to its actions in the first revolution in 2011, the army did not assume political control of the transition, but immediately presented a civil president and cabinet. However, it is clear that the army continues to play an important role in Egypt, politically and economically, as it has for the past 60 years. Particularly in foreign policy, it remains the military that sets out the boundaries.

The massacre[10] of protesting Muslim Brothers committed by the military raises serious questions of accountability though. Can anyone really hold the military accountable? Or does the army remain an untouchable state within the state? As was the case in Malaysia and Turkey, it will probably take considerable time for the Egyptian army to be reined in to its appropriate role.

The most important question, however, is what will happen to the MB. Up to today, they still refuse to accept Morsi's removal and refuse to talk unless he is restored to office. We will undoubtedly see more clashes in the weeks and months to come. Still, overtures for talks – whether or not under the auspices of the EU – remain possible. In any case, for Egypt to make progress, it is necessary to find some sort of democratic modus vivendi. For this to happen, hate and mistrust will have to make way for something we, in all democratic countries, learned to live with a long time ago: compromise.

---

10 This is a reference to the killing of at least 51 Muslim Brothers in the morning of 8 July 2013 at the Club of the Republican Guards in Cairo, when the police cleared a sit-in of people protesting the removal of president Morsi. The massacre in Rabaa, where hundreds of Muslim Brothers were killed happened later, on 14 August 2013. Also see '16. Egypt: will there be order after the chaos? An outsider's perspective' (10 July 2013)

18. What should the EU decide on Egypt?
Published on *EU Observer*, 20 September 2013

I came back to Egypt a few days after 14 August, when hundreds of Muslim Brothers were killed in Rabaa, a neighbourhood in Cairo. We will probably never know what exactly happened that day. The army says that snipers killed one of their officers and that Muslim Brothers were shooting their own people. Muslim Brothers say they were slaughtered while protesting peacefully. Obviously there was a lot of tension in Egypt and being convinced of their side of the story, the Egyptian government didn't accept any criticism. It was in this atmosphere that I tried to formulate an advice to the European Union on how to react to this situation.

I arrived back in Cairo late in the evening, during curfew. The streets were as good as empty and the soldiers at the checkpoints were fairly friendly. However, in the distance I could hear gunshots. Apparently, at some checkpoints soldiers fire into the air to warn people that a checkpoint is on the way. Another sign of the tense situation. My taxi driver told me that his pro-Morsi friends will not stop fighting, a fact he deplores. In his opinion, it is up to the Muslim Brotherhood to refrain from violence first.

Both the Muslim Brotherhood and the secular/military side are very much convinced of the truth of their story. Moreover, for many Egyptians, the current battle is one of life and death. It is a struggle for the identity of their country and what they believe in. No wonder that the emotions run very, very deep. In the past two months, the battle has wrecked many friendship and even families. Whoever makes a remark that goes against one of the two stories is rubberstamped as a traitor and an apologist of the rival camp. This state of mind – on top of the historical allergy to any foreign interference – makes most Egyptians today oversensitive to any remarks from the international community.

The result of this 'you are either with us or against us' mindset is that every country has been put in one of the camps. So far, Turkey, Tunisia, Qatar, Malaysia and Germany have been put in the pro-Morsi camp. Saudi-Arabia, Kuwait, Bahrain, Jordan, the UAE and Russia are in the anti-Morsi camp. The United States is a kind of special case as both camps are convinced the US is supporting the other side. One could of course discuss whether all this is fair or not, but what I am trying to do is explain the current Egyptian state of mind.

An important question is who in the international community is left to mediate between the two camps. I see only the European Union as a possible candidate. The access granted on both sides to the EU High Representative surprised everyone. It was General Sisi who gave her permission to meet with Morsi. It was through the EU that, after April 2013, Egypt came close to a negotiated way out of the crisis. If Morsi had accepted this first deal, he would still be president, be it of a united government. If the Army had accepted the second deal (in August), the bloody dispersal of Rabaa on 14 August most probably would not have taken place.

Although I understand that, for the voters back home, it is good for the European governments to take some measures against Egypt, I think it is important for the EU to think about two questions: What is the impact of a decision and what are the consequences?

What is the impact? The European Union can take several measures. It can cut the budget lines of the EU Neighbourhood Policy[1]. It can combine this with cutting the aid from the EU member states. And it can cut or freeze the economic boost promised in November 2012. About how much money are we talking? The budget of the EU Neighbourhood Policy is less than €200 million a year. Combined with the national budgets for aid to Egypt, we are talking about €600 million, more or less.

These are fairly small budgets. Moreover, given the situation, most of that money is not being spent. The economic boost budget would be €5 billion. This is of course significant, but we have to take into account that this amount is merely offered via loans that have to be paid back. If we compare these amounts with the $12 billion promised by Saudi Arabia, Kuwait and the UAE, we must admit that the impact of cutting these budgets is fairly limited. On top of that, Saudi Arabia has already promised they will step in and pay for any aid cut by the West.

---

1   The European Neighbourhood Policy is the umbrella of all programs of the European Commission that deal with countries close to the EU but that cannot become members of the EU. The program is divided between the Eastern Neighbourhood (Belarus, Moldova, Ukraine, Georgia, Armenia and Azerbaijan) and the Southern Neighbourhood or the Arab world and Israel. In November 2012, the EU renamed its efforts as EU-Egypt Task Force. See '1. EU-Egypt Task Force: the perfect misunderstanding' (15 November 2012). See also the preface by Guy Verhofstadt.

Other possible measures could be an arms embargo, or a travel ban for certain persons. Although the EU itself has of course no arm deals with Egypt, the member states do. All arm contracts together are worth a few hundred million euros. The problem with an embargo, as well as with travel bans, is that it smells too much of what the EU did in Syria. The fact that Russia would be happy to take over these contracts sounds even more like the Syrian outcome.

But even more important than the numbers is the fact that it is very unlikely that one or both camps will change its position or the way it works due to any of these measures. No country likes to be punished, but if punishments do not change anything then why take these measures? Some say that remaining silent would be even worse. I agree, but I think we should first look at the possible consequences.

What are the consequences? The main consequence of taking tough measures against Egypt today could be that the EU is placed in the pro-Morsi camp. The EU can of course say that it remains neutral and wants merely to stop giving aid to a country that uses violence against its citizens. But that would not work for the anti-Morsi side. The most problematic consequence of this would be that the European Union loses its neutrality and thus its ability to mediate. And as the EU is left as the only possible mediator, that could be problematic in the near future, as there is no scenario in which Egypt can stabilize and go forward without a solution for both camps.

The EU can – and should – of course condemn the violence committed by both sides. The police reaction to the sit-in at Rabaa was disproportionate and thus unacceptable. But arming protesters and burning churches is no less unacceptable. The EU can add new conditions to its aid and economic boost package. It is necessary to get proof from the Egyptian government that it is heading towards elections that are open for all and that human rights are being respected. But if the EU wants to keep its important role as future mediator, it should resist the calls from the public back home to immediately take severe measures against Egypt.

TUNISIA
Some reflections

I am writing this on 14 January 2014, exactly three years after Tunisian president Ben Ali fled the country after almost a month of protests throughout Tunisia. It all started when fruit vendor Mohamed Bouazizi set himself on fire after the police confiscated his wares. The world, and certainly the Arab world, was stunned. Suddenly it seemed possible for people to set in motion *real* change.

Tunisia was the first Arab Spring country to organize elections. On 22 November 2011, I went to Tunis to observe the unfolding of these elections. It was a magical experience. I have never seen people so happy about being able to vote in free and fair elections. They waited for hours to cast their ballot. On exiting the polling station, they took pictures of themselves proudly pointing their painted finger… Moving moments for every genuine democrat.

In the evening, however, the magic turned sour: all indications showed at least a 40 percent win for Ennahda, the Tunisian version of the Muslim Brotherhood. I immediately realized that 40 percent for Islamists in a secular country like Tunisia would mean 60 percent and more in Egypt. It was a hard wake-up call from a perhaps naïve dream that the Arab Revolution would directly lead to a secular, liberal democracy.

The political story of Tunisia and Egypt after the Revolution followed a similar track. In both countries, a transition government prepared for elections that ended up a major victory for the Muslim Brotherhood. Both constitutional processes suffered as Islamists wanted too much 'Islam' in it. In both countries, the popularity of the Islamists faltered, leading to new protests and, finally, the end of their power. The main differences between the countries are that the Muslim Brotherhood in Egypt is much bigger than its Tunisian counterpart, that the people in Egypt are less educated and that the reaction against the Muslim Brotherhood finally led to the dissolution of the entire organization.

In Tunisia, politics is in general more 'civilized'. Even though two major opposition politicians[1] were assassinated, violence is fairly rare. Tunisia was also lucky that the fundamentals of its economy were strong when the Tunisians inherited the country from presidents Zine Al Abidine Ben Ali and Habib Bourguiba. Egypt, on the contrary, was (and still is) bankrupt.

---

1 In 2013 Chokri Belaid and Mohamed Brahmi were assassinated. The minister of interior said it was done by the same killer, with the same gun. Both were leaders of the leftish Popular Front coalition. Ennahda was blamed by many for being behind the assassinations.

Tunisia has also always been more open, more directed towards Europe and more intellectually and politically mature.

There is no doubt that Tunisia will be the first real liberal democracy of the Arab Spring countries, even if the way there has its ups and downs. Just as it was the country that sparked the Arab Revolution, it will remain an example of good practice. And because it is doing so much better than Egypt, Libya, Yemen or Syria, it tends not to be mentioned often in Western newspapers. I too must admit that my reports on Tunisia were usually not longer than a few paragraphs with updates. Indeed, I apologize in advance that even this piece on Tunisia – a report to the ALDE – talks largely about Egypt.

1. Political fight for power in Egypt and Tunisia
ALDE Report, 10 November 2012

It is interesting to see how Egypt and Tunisia are following a similar path. In both countries, the Muslim Brothers/Ennahda won the elections and are dominant in the government. Both are working on the Constitution, a process that takes longer than expected and highlights severe political clashes between the Salafis[1] and the seculars, with the MB/Ennahda in the middle. In both states, liberal opposition groups are uniting, finding hope in the declining popularity of the MB/Ennahda. It is also interesting to see that both MB and Ennahda don't really know how to deal with the Salafi opposition. This can be compared with the doubting stance many European conservative parties took, and are still taking, towards the far right, out of fear for their voters. In Tunisia and Egypt, the more moderate Islamist parties fear that people will consider the Salafis as 'better Muslims', as the former, being in government, have to make compromises. That is the reason why, behind closed doors, many leaders from MB/Ennahda are speaking Salafi language, which – especially if leaked, as in the case of Gannouchi – is embarrassing for their international image. At the same time, we see in both countries that the liberal opposition is struggling with their identity. They know what they don't want – the 'Islamisation' of their country – but they have trouble making clear what they do want. Words like 'secular' or 'liberal' can easily sound atheist or anti-Islam, an image that guarantees electoral defeat.

I was in Tunisia last week and I met with the main players of the social-liberal El Joumhouri party: Néguib Chebbi, Maya Jribi and Yassine Brahim. Although there are no credible opinion polls in Tunisia, they are all pointing in the same direction. According to these polls, Ennahda has lost one third to half of their voters. The party of President Moncef Marzouki hardly exists anymore, while the other partner in the coalition government, the socialist Ettakatol, has also been decimated. El Joumhouri ends as the

---

[1] The Salafis (very conservative Islamists) are not as strong in Tunisia as they are in Egypt. However, they created a lot of unrest and riots and declared some places as independent emirates. They are feared and hated by many Tunisians.

third party. The second biggest party – or maybe the first – is the new party of former prime minister Essebsi. Beji Caid Essebsi was Prime Minister of the transitional government after the Tunisian revolution. Although he is 86 years old, people see him as an efficient politician. The popularity of his party is focused on his personality, rather than on the party. That is why the well-organized El Joumhouri party and Essebsi are looking into ways of cooperating or forming an alliance to defeat Ennahda in the next elections. The question, however, is when these elections will take place.

I also visited the Constituent Assembly, where the debate on the draft constitution had just started. I met with several secular members of the Assembly who seemed to be quite confident about the eventual outcome of the constitution. The fact that Salafis burned a part of the US Embassy and the American College (I saw the remaining traces of the fire) as a reaction to the so-called Mohamed movie (making jokes about the Prophet), weakened their political position. I was also asked to attend a press conference that announced the end of a hunger strike of two MPs against the possibility of former *Rassemblement Constitutionnel Démocratique* (RCD) members being allowed to participate in politics. Another main point of discussion is whether the presidential elections should be held simultaneously with the parliamentary ones or not.

In Egypt, too, the fight over the constitution is intensifying. Contrary to Tunisia, the Salafi parties hold considerable weight in the Constitutional Committee. The ideology of the Salafi movement is pretty simple: they want to live exactly like the Prophet Mohamed did and organise society based on the Koran. Many of their proposals for the constitution are ludicrous. The leader of the Salafist Nour party wanted to put the marriageable age for women at nine, because of a (supposed) phrase in the Koran. They also wanted to restrict equality between men and women by adding "as long as it does not contradict with the rules of the Sharia". Last Friday, there was a demonstration on Tahrir in support of the full implementation of Sharia in the constitution. I went to take a look and found many Saudi and only a few Egyptian flags. The demonstration was neither supported by the MB nor by the official Salafi parties. Nevertheless, there were some 40,000 people present. The MB is constantly mediating between these extreme proposals and the outraged liberals.

As many liberal representatives have quit the Constitutional Committee in Egypt[2], the main 'secular' work is done by Amr Moussa and Ayman

---

2   See footnote page 97.

Nour. This weekend, Moussa introduced amendments to 200 articles. He also announced he would walk out, with 30 other members, if the process was done in a hurry. At the same time, there is a struggle between the Constitutional Committee and the judges. The draft constitution would limit the power of the Constitutional Court, giving the president more power to appoint some important judges and prosecutors. The judges have reacted vehemently and threatened not to oversee the referendum, which should be held two weeks after the draft constitution is ready. There also remains a possibility that the Constitutional Court will dissolve the Committee as it could be judged unconstitutional. The Committee was appointed by the same parliament that was ruled unconstitutional by the Constitutional Court[3]. In short, there is a fight between those who want this draft constitution finished as soon as possible (MB, as well as the Salafis) and those who want a new start (Baradei, Sabahi, Constitutional Court). The question is: is it true or not that Moussa and Nour are delaying the drafting process in silent support for the second camp? In any case, a delay would help the new liberal alliances to build their support. As elections should be held two months after the referendum (so, February), a delay of a few months would give them more breathing space.

In the meantime, the government in Egypt is losing its authority. They have not managed to get control over Sinai and are also taken less and less seriously by the people. The most controversial decision they have taken is to impose a closing hour on shops and restaurants. The reason for the decision is that Egypt is dealing with a serious energy problem while simultaneously heavily subsidizing this energy. As a result, the government decided that shops should close at 10 pm, restaurants at 12 am. For most Europeans, this sounds more than reasonable. However, Cairo is a city that never sleeps. Carrefour, for example, is open until 4 am. There are even areas where the shops don't have doors as they never close. As it is impossible to implement, the government decided to postpone the decision and to make it midnight for shops and 2 am for restaurants. But even that will prove to be impossible to implement. Another example of declining authority is the decision by the prosecutor to forbid pornographic material on the Internet. Not only is it strange for a prosecutor to impose this, but it is also not possible to implement. This ruling is likely another example of how the courts are trying to weaken the

---

3   See 'II. Belgium: unconstitutional parliament for 10 years and still rolling!' (9 July 2012)

government and the Muslim Brotherhood. It might also be out of revenge for the fact that President Morsi tried to fire the prosecutor-general and make him ambassador to the Vatican. The prosecutor-general refused (as did the 'Club of Judges'), because, he said, the president has no authority over the judiciary.

Another important element in the current state of play is the election of Tawadros III as the new Coptic pope. He has said that he will not interfere in politics… "Politics is a dirty word to us, and we do not think it should be mixed with religion."[4] This is the complete opposite line to the one taken by the former pope, Shenouda, who played the role of political representative of the Copts. He made the major mistake of forbidding the Coptic youth from attending the 25 January 2011 revolution on Tahrir Square for political reasons. This mixing of religion and politics has been one of the reasons for the increasing difficulties of Copts in Egyptian society. It will be interesting to see how the new position of the pope changes the Muslim-Coptic paradigm in Egypt. This too is one of the many elements below the surface, elements that don't make it onto the News, but that will shape Egypt in the years and decades to come.

---

4 *New York Times*, 4 November 2012: http://www.nytimes.com/2012/11/05/world/middleeast/coptic-church-chooses-pope-who-rejects-politics.html

SYRIA
Reflections from May 2012
to January 2014

I have visited Syria six times: three times before and three times during the revolution that started on 15 March 2011. One of my best friends lived in Damascus. I saw (and adored) Aleppo, Daraa, Maloula, Deir Ezzor and Homs and it was my visit to the famous Umayyad mosque in Damascus that changed my view of Islam. Like most in the West, I had thought of Islam as the religion of the sword, of tension and fanaticism. When I entered this 1300-year old mosque, I felt none of that. On the contrary, families were picnicking; children were playing, while adults prayed; others were just taking a nap. It was an oasis of peace.

I joined the famous poetry nights in Damascus where everything was acceptable as long as you didn't criticize Bashar Al Assad's regime. The regime was the only thing I disliked about Syria. Huge pictures of Bashar and his father, Hafez, were ubiquitous. The only reason I was relieved to cross the border with Lebanon again was to escape the omnipresence of Assad and the fear of his repression.

The revolution in Syria started in March 2011, when a few kids plastered the Tunisian slogan "Down, down with the regime" across a wall in Daraa, a city south of Damascus. The secret police (Mukhabarat) arrested the kids. Their parents visited the prison to ask for their release and they were let out after a few days. They had been tortured, their nails pulled out of their fingers and toes. This was the catalyst for the protests, which began on 15 March.

But Bashar Al Assad followed the same credo as his father: no mercy. Peaceful protesters were immediately arrested, imprisoned and tortured or just executed. After a few months, citizens decided to get organized to defend their families. Following their conscience, soldiers started to defect, founding the Free Syrian Army (FSA). Following the Libyan example, opposition forces tried to form a united Syrian National Council (SNC).

On 24 February 2012, 70 countries came together in Gammarth, Tunisia, for the first meeting of the Friends of Syria. Although I was not part of any official delegation, I went as well, putting some opposition representatives in contact with top European diplomats. European rejection of the FSA's demands for support and weapons to protect its people was defended for three reasons:

1. There is no guarantee that, after Assad, a sectarian war will not break out.
2. We are not convinced there is, as yet, an alternative to Assad.
3. We cannot be sure that weapons will not fall into the wrong hands.

Jabhat Al Nusra, the first jihadist group in Syria, was only one month old at this stage. There were no foreign Jihadis and no trace of Al Qaeda in Syria whatsoever. The European stance could have been the first paragraphs of a chapter in Barbara Tuchman's *The March of Folly*. Hesitation from the international community created the space for jihadist forces to grow and for Assad to continue – and intensify – his crimes against humanity.

I witnessed the results during my three visits to Syria in 2013. Smuggled through its border with Turkey, I saw the destruction, the inequality of power on the battlefield and the human suffering with my own eyes. I cried for the first time in many years. I was ashamed to be part of an international community that was not doing anything to help the Syrian people.

After my first visit, on the plane back to Cairo, I began my report for the ALDE Group on the country's humanitarian disaster, as well as the total lack of aid in Northern Aleppo. Many people were shocked when they read the report and started spreading it around. The report was discussed in the European, Dutch, Belgian and German parliaments. I also rewrote it for the Carnegie Endowment for International Peace. The facts I presented annoyed both the European bureaucracy and the International Committee of the Red Cross. I was accused in an official letter by the Dutch minister of humanitarian aid of bringing the lives of aid workers in Syria into danger.

On my return to Syria in February I met with the General Commander of the Free Syrian Army, Salim Idriss. He didn't look like the rebel commander I had expected. He was gentle, soft spoken and a good listener. ALDE president Guy Verhofstadt immediately agreed to invite him to the European Parliament to make his case. On 6 March 2012, Idriss made his first public appearance, surprising everyone with his moderate stance and rational argumentation.

Three weeks later, I was invited, together with two Syrian friends and activists, Rami Jarrah (better known under his alias, Alexander Page) and Deiaa Dughmoch, to the FSA headquarters. I believe I was the first foreigner to spend time there (I even spent the night). We were privileged to see how the organization functioned with its rudimentary means.

This experience, as well as my previous meetings with the Free Syrian Army commanders, gave me unique insights and the opportunity to write with authority on the FSA: what it is, how it is organized and what their strengths and weaknesses are. One of the pieces ('The FSA does exist') was published, republished and spread all over the Internet garnering plenty of attention in Washington in particular. Some say it changed the way DC looked at Idriss and the FSA, although this is hard to verify. In any case, it didn't change Western policy on the ground…

Out of all the countries of the Arab Revolution, Syria is the one that keeps us awake the most at night. By 'us', I mean (almost all) the analysts and journalists who follow the Arab world. Across the world, people are feeling increasingly confused about what is happening in Syria and increasingly tired of seeing disturbing pictures of killed children, destroyed cities and shouting jihadists. Nonetheless, we see it as our duty to keep reporting on, and explaining, what is going on in Syria. It is the least the Syrians deserve.

1. Syria is a second Bosnia. Assad is Milošević
Published on *EU Observer*, 29 May 2012

The conflict in Syria was and still is confusing for most people. The large amount of propaganda, lies and brutal videos leave even many decision makers unsecure about what exactly was happening. One of the reasons of this confusion is that very few of them have ever been in Syria. Contrary to many other conflicts, there is hardly any emotional connection to the country. I tried to make things more understandable by comparing the conflict in Syria with the war in Bosnia. I (wrongly) hoped it would push the international community to take action and stop this human catastrophe.

We all saw the horrifying images: dozens of children who were mercilessly slaughtered in the Syrian city of Houla[1]. This is just one of the many massacres since the Syrian revolution started on 15 March 2011. Men, women, children are killed by the regime's soldiers by grenades, bullets, knives or bare hands. Those who are captured are tortured to death in the most brutal ways. We all know it. We all see it. But the focus on Syria is fading. It's hard to broadcast the same news every day. Meanwhile, the international community keeps on 'observing'. It's a crying shame. How much longer are we going to leave Bashar Al-Assad untouched?

Although cynical, the comparison with the war in Bosnia is more than merited. The situation is nearly identical. A quick memory refresher: the violence in Bosnia started in April 1992, after the disintegration of Yugoslavia. The Bosnian Serbs proclaimed their own republic and carried out an ethnic cleansing through the whole territory, mainly of Bosnian Muslims, which led to 100,000 victims. The most horrifying images, especially those of Sarajevo and Srebrenica, remain deeply embedded in our minds. This is one of the darkest pages in the history of the international community.

---

1   On 25 May 2012, two opposition-controlled villages in the Houla region of Syria were attacked by pro-government thugs (Shabiha). According to the United Nations, 108 people were killed, including 34 women and 49 children.

Why? As in Syria, the international community tried a peace plan for Bosnia. This was on 1 May 1993, also 13 months after the war and the slaughtering had started. The plan required that the Serbs stop shelling Sarajevo. The comparison with Homs and Hama is clear. When the horror continued, Western countries scanned each other for months to measure their readiness for a military intervention. Alas, nobody was ready. The reasons for their hesitance will sound familiar: the situation was complex; it was a sectarian war between Orthodox, Catholics and Muslims who had all committed crimes, which made it difficult to choose a side; Russia was objecting because of its ties with Serbia; and there was "no post-war-plan".

Only three years and 100,000 victims after the beginning of the war did military intervention finally take place. A few months after the intervention, the Dayton agreements were signed by all parties concerned. Bosnia had to wait until the ethnic massacre of Srebrenica, where 7,000 Bosnians were murdered at once (while they were under UN protection), to receive this outcome.

It is a disgrace that the international community is using identical reasons for not intervening in Syria. The situation is complex in Syria; there is fear of sectarian violence; Russia is objecting; there is no "post-Assad plan" and the opposition is divided – even if they are united in the request for Assad to leave. Since 2001, there has been another argument, cunningly manipulated by Assad: the presence of Al-Qaeda. Although we can doubt to what extent Al-Qaeda still exists, since a few months ago there are indeed members present in Syria. That was the case in Bosnia as well, and there are probably as many of them in Syria as there used to be in Bosnia at the time: a few hundred. The only difference is that back then they were called Mujahedeen.

In Cairo I regularly meet Syrian opposition leaders. Each of them fled Syria during the past six months. Many of them lived underground for months. Others were tortured in Assad's prisons. They all say the same thing: after the massacre in Houla it should be clear to everybody that Kofi Annan's peace plan doesn't work and will never work. Assad will do everything to stay in power … His army will continue to rape, to kill and to destroy. His secret service will continue to arrest people who dare to talk to UN observers and torture them to death. Those who openly oppose Assad will be killed (often along with their entire family). The terror will remain, even though Assad is not in a strong position at all. That part of the army fighting for him consists of only 20,000 soldiers. He doesn't trust the others. More than 100,000 soldiers are kept in their barracks. Last week, I heard from somebody who had just fled Damascus that Assad has confiscated passports of ministers and army generals, to prevent them from escaping the country.

There is only one way to stop this terror and that is with an international intervention and the creation of one or two safe zones where people can find refuge and from where humanitarian aid can be sent to the right places. Sooner or later, this intervention will take place, just as it did in Bosnia. With the UN if possible, with NATO if necessary, just like in Kosovo in 1999. The only question is: how many more children will need to be massacred before proper action is taken?

2. Eyewitness account – Syria: a report from the field
Published by the Carnegie Endowment for International Peace, 14 February 2013

This is a rare, personal report of a trip into Syria's beleaguered provinces. Koert Debeuf, a Belgian working for the European Parliament, travelled with commanders of the rebel Free Syrian Army into the Aleppo region. Back from "the hell called Syria," to use Debeuf's own words, he describes his impressions and conclusions from talks with soldiers, civilians, and refugees.

From 18 to 23 January, I visited Turkey and the Aleppo region of northern Syria. In the city of Antakya in southern Turkey – known in ancient times as Antioch – I met commanders of the Free Syrian Army (FSA) and people responsible for distributing humanitarian aid in those regions. They gave us a very good overview of the situation on the ground.

On 21 January, we went into Syria with General Abdel Nasser Farzat, the FSA commander for the Aleppo region. As the Bab al-Salam border crossing was temporarily closed, we were smuggled into the country. Using minor roads to avoid shelling and regime soldiers who still occupy a few strongholds in the Aleppo region, we arrived at about 8 pm in Azaz at the house of an FSA officer who offered us a meal. After dinner we headed to the headquarters where we met Ahmed Abeit, the commander of the revolutionary High Council of the Military Council.

It was clear from the beginning of our trip that nobody really knows who has exactly which function in the military opposition. There are two overlapping structures: the FSA – dominated by former generals from the Syrian regime army – and the revolutionary forces. Both have commanders; they work together but the hierarchy is unclear. Ahmed Abeit told us that he had been elected general commander of the revolutionary structure for the whole of Syria. The next day, when we visited the battlefield at Quweris airport, we saw Abeit again and realized he really was in charge.

A deep distrust of the West

It was not easy talking to the senior commanders. They are deeply suspicious about anything European or American. Every one of them kept repeating how they have seen nothing at all materialize from the many promises that were made by the international community. We – the international community – promised them support if they organized themselves militarily. Nothing came. We asked them to organize civilian councils. Nothing came. We promised them humanitarian aid. Nothing came. We promised weapons. Nothing came. Every single one of these commanders is convinced that the West is on the side of President Bashar al-Assad, and it is very difficult to disprove these accusations.

Despite the distrust, they did appreciate that I had come. Because of security concerns – mainly a fear of kidnapping – only the most senior officers knew that I work at the European Parliament. They were glad that at least one European official had made the effort to come to the region and was trying to help (without promising anything). After a conversation of about two hours, we went back to the officer's house in Azaz, where the four of us, and the general, slept on the living room floor. That night we heard bombs being dropped from planes on a neighbouring town. The officer said it was most likely the bombing would reach Azaz by morning. Luckily that didn't happen.

A visit to a battlefield

The next morning we thought the general would take us by car to Aleppo. Instead, he brought us to the battlefield at Quweris airport. They told us it was safe, but we heard and saw continuous shelling and gunfire. We had to run or walk quickly from place to place. The area had been captured the day before, and the rebels were preparing for a big battle to seize the airport. To prevent the regime forces from taking back any ground – about 2,000 soldiers were stuck at the airport – the FSA fired bombs from where we stood. I saw with my own eyes what Ahmed Abeit had told me the day before: the FSA has to build bombs and equipment from whatever metal it can find because it doesn't receive any serious weapons from abroad. This is in sharp contrast to the cluster bombs and other huge explosives I saw fired by the regime. The FSA has no anti-aircraft guns either, so they have no way of stopping the continuous random shelling of the civilian population.

I visited a small division at the frontline from where I saw three bombs being fired at the airport. Although the soldiers were proud to demonstrate their fighting skills, their commander told me they were sad to be fighting at all. He said the FSA wanted peace, but that it was Assad who had forced them into war. He gave me an olive branch and asked me to take it to the European Parliament to show Europe that the FSA's intentions were good.

Bombing the bakeries

I felt relieved when we left the battlefield. We went back to Azaz, where we saw the only bakery that was still in operation; the regime is deliberately bombing bakeries in order to hurt the population. Even worse was the marketplace we visited: one week earlier, at 2 pm, the most crowded time on market day, the regime had shelled the marketplace with two huge missiles. Thirty people of all ages were killed immediately, and 300 were seriously injured. The place was razed to the ground.

Desperate local people told me that there were still bodies under the rubble, but that they lacked the equipment to dig them out. They blame the EU and the United States for doing nothing and for not helping them in any way. There is no food, no medical aid, no electricity, and almost no heating. It is hard to describe the frustration, the pain, and the shame I felt at that marketplace.

The Azaz refugee camp

The shortage of humanitarian aid in the refugee camps is shocking. I visited the camp at Azaz in the Aleppo region. Almost no aid reaches this place, even though it would be perfectly safe to bring in food and supplies. The camp is located only a few hundred meters from the Bab al-Salam crossing on the Turkish border where no trucks were waiting. I even saw a Turkish ambulance pass right by the camp on its way from Syria back into Turkey.

There are 11,400 people living in the camp, initially built for a few hundred. Eight thousand of these are children. Yet the storage room for milk is empty. The camp does receive some milk, but not nearly enough.

So for every few days of milk, there are two weeks of no milk. The lack of food is so serious that people in the camp only get one meal a day. Even then, the supplies were only going to last another two days after our visit. When I asked the director whether more food would arrive soon, he said he could only hope for that.

A humanitarian disaster

There is a serious lack of heating. On the day we visited the camp, four children died because of the cold. Some tents have no heating – I saw a family with a disabled child in such a tent – others have only a small coal stove. The tents are, of course, small (9 square metres), and families are usually large (between six and 10 people). Because of the rain, the tents are wet underneath, and water and mud runs between them. Due to the lack of toilets, parts of the camp have become an open sewer, which leads to a high risk of epidemics. Disease has already broken out in one camp. There is rarely any electricity. There is no medicine and almost no medical support. I saw a 12-month-old boy with an open shrapnel wound on his leg. It hadn't been treated for days. His desperate father came out of one of the unheated tents in the mud to show him to me.

My conclusion is that the Syrians I spoke to are right: there is no support whatsoever going to the 'liberated areas'. In terms of territory, the FSA controls about 75 percent of Syria. In terms of people, it is hard to tell, but probably about half of the population lives in 'liberated areas'. The humanitarian situation is incredibly dramatic. It is such a disaster that it is hard to describe or even imagine.

My summary

I would summarize the situation as follows:

1. There is very little aid coming to the 'liberated' (FSA-controlled) areas. Every commander and council leader I spoke to confirmed that the only aid they receive comes from Turkey, Qatar, Saudi Arabia, or smaller, mostly private organizations. The only major organization represented is Médecins Sans Frontières, which has three small field hospitals in the Aleppo region.

2. There is no aid coming to these 'liberated areas' through the Syrian Red Cross. Assad's regime is doing its utmost to prevent aid from reaching his opponents. The director of the Azaz camp told me that all he had ever received through official channels were some rubber sleeping mats – and that was a long time ago. The fact that the UN announced this week that it would give the Syrian Red Cross 519 million dollars to help all the people of Syria, caused huge outrage in the Aleppo region.
3. Contrary to rumours, Turkey did not close its border permanently. I have seen about 100 trucks with aid waiting to enter Syria, and Turkey decides when it is safe enough for them to go in. Turkey is the one country that is helping the Syrians.
4. Contrary to their image, the 'liberated areas' are organized. In every area except Homs, there is a military council, a civilian council, a court, and a police force. The main reasons they can't do more are the continuous shelling and the lack of humanitarian aid. People are so desperate that there is a lot of theft. Because of the shelling, it is also hard for the police and the judiciary to concentrate on law and order. The lack of humanitarian aid weakens the authority of these councils because they can't provide people with the absolute basics of food and medicine.

What should be done

It is clear that many people will die if humanitarian aid does not reach the FSA-controlled areas quickly. The aid promised by the United Nations Office for the Coordination of Humanitarian Affairs to the Syrian Red Cross will not reach these places, whatever the Syrian government may promise. For getting aid to the right areas and the right people, we have to differentiate between two situations:

The camps close to the Turkish-Syrian border – as well as those inside Turkey – should be provided with aid directly, as there is no security problem and it is not true that the border is closed. This can be done through the Turkish Red Crescent or similar organizations. Aside from bureaucracy, I see no obstacle in getting aid to these camps.

There is also a solution for aid that has to go deeper into Syria. There is already a network in place that brings aid from Turkey to various rebel-held areas and even to Homs, which is surrounded by regime forces. This network is organized by the civil councils of the rebel cities and towns and enjoys the protection of the FSA.

A leap of faith

I have convinced the two commanders, Abdel Nasser Farzat and Ahmed Abeit, to appoint civilians to manage aid efforts. This wasn't easy, as both are very cynical about the West. They have given me one chance to try again. The person or unit they appoint will work with the connections that already exist and represent the civilian councils to make sure that every aid package will go where it was meant to go.

If the EU really wants to help the Syrian people, it should use this setup, even if it needs to take a leap of faith to do so. The EU also urgently needs to convince the international humanitarian community to take the same leap of faith. If this is impossible, another way must be found. Urgently.

The political dimension is also important. The FSA and the civilian councils are losing respect and authority because they cannot deliver aid. That is why people are increasingly following the jihadists and al-Qaeda. If we fail to deliver on the humanitarian level as we did in the past on the political and military level, we should not be surprised if post-Assad Syria becomes even more anti-Western than the country has been under the current regime.

3. Syrian insurgents say aid isn't getting where it needs to go
Article in the *International New York Times*
by Kristen McTighe, 6 March 2013

This article was published in the International New York Times *(then International Herald Tribune) on the day that Salim Idriss, General Commander of the FSA, visited the ALDE Group in the European Parliament. Kristen McTighe, a freelance journalist for the* New York Times *in Cairo, approached me after having read my eyewitness account.*

CAIRO — Koert Debeuf, a Belgian who works in Cairo as a representative of centrist parties in the European Parliament, says he was smuggled from Turkey into Syria by rebel commanders in January to study conditions in the rebel-held territories. But when he asked the commanders to show him the Azaz refugee camp in northern Aleppo Province, he said he had the impression that they felt ashamed.

"They were too proud to ask us to help them with aid or weapons, and it was as if showing us the misery would have been like admitting their own failures as the FSA," Mr. Debeuf said, referring to the Free Syrian Army, a loose coalition of armed rebels.

When he persisted and was finally allowed to enter the camp, he said, it was he who was left feeling embarrassed because of the squalor and the fact that so little help from Europe was reaching the people there.

"I felt so ashamed to be European. It was very emotional. I was very angry," he said during an interview last month in Cairo. "The whole thing is just so unjust, so inhumane."

In what has been called one of the worst humanitarian situations produced by the civil war, international humanitarian aid has largely failed to reach camps in rebel strongholds, leaving internally displaced Syrians living in squalor just meters from the Turkish border.

"The humanitarian aid is coming through the regime" of president Bashar al-Assad, said the rebel Gen. Salim Idris, chief of staff of the FSA, on Tuesday by telephone from Brussels. "It is coming through the Syrian Red Crescent, and only a little of this is coming to the liberated areas."

During his visit, the first by a rebel commander to the European capital, General Idris accused the Syrian regime of blocking international aid from reaching rebel-held areas, and he called on Europe to provide direct humanitarian aid through the rebel command organization.

"We have the structures needed to receive this aid to get it to the liberated areas, to the people who need it," General Idris said.

The next day, addressing a meeting of Mr. Debeuf's group, the Alliance of Liberals and Democrats for Europe, or ALDE, at the European Parliament, General Idris said the rebel army controlled as much as 70 percent of certain regions of Syria. He also said that if the FSA were given sufficient support, radical units like the jihadist Al-Nusra Front, a Sunni insurgent force that US officials have blacklisted as a terrorist organization, would become irrelevant.

General Idris said there were five million civilian refugees in Syria, and he condemned the lack of humanitarian aid from the West. "We look to people in the west as our brothers in humanity, but people in Syria say that the international community just looks at the TV screens, says Assad should go – but does not act," he said.

In January, with two Syrian activists based in Cairo and a guide, Mr. Debeuf travelled with commanders of the FSA into Aleppo Province at his own initiative, he said, to see first-hand what was happening.

The Azaz camp, he said, "was the worst thing I've seen in my life".

Built for only a few hundred refugees, numbers at the camp in northern Aleppo had grown to more than 11,000, including more than 8,000 children. With no heat, no electricity and no running water, families were crammed into tents and children were infested with lice.

The room designed to store milk was empty, he said, and babies as young as three months had only sugar water to drink. Food was scarce and meals were rationed to one per day. In two days, food was set to run out.

Inside one tent, he saw a disabled girl lying motionless on the ground. She suffered from epilepsy and needed medicine. In another tent, he met a father holding his year-old son. While fleeing their home, the child's leg had been ripped open by shrapnel and it was clear, Mr. Debeuf said, that if the child did not receive treatment soon, he would die. That day alone, Mr. Debeuf was told, four children had died from cold.

Mr. Debeuf said people in the camp were angry: "Every single one of them was convinced that we were supporting Assad, and if you are there, what can you say? There was $519 million in aid promised and they've got nothing."

That was a reference to developments in January, when donors pledged $1.5 billion in assistance to UN humanitarian agencies, with $519 million being requested for humanitarian aid to those inside the country. The United Nations, which works with various partners, including international and national non-government organizations, has repeatedly stressed the need for humanitarian operations to remain neutral and to avoid politicization.

But according to UN rules, NGO's and their partners in Syria must be authorized to work by the Syrian government. That has brought accusations from the rebels that aid is being unequally distributed.

"Some in the opposition have criticized this, saying the UN is funding the regime," said Omar Hossino, a Syrian-American researcher based in Washington, who recently visited the rebel-held northern regions.

"That is an exaggeration," he said: "but there is a legitimacy to those critiques. If you are going to be an NGO, national or international, authorized by the Syrian government, you are going to be under strict restrictions."

At the center of criticism has been the Syrian Red Crescent, one of the main UN partners in distributing aid. General Idris and others in opposition strongholds have accused it of unequal distribution, favouring supporters of the regime.

But with the situation on the ground already perilous, others say the accusations are unfair and risk putting aid workers at an even greater risk of becoming targets. Aid workers of the Syrian Red Crescent have been killed by both government and opposition forces, and some have reportedly been imprisoned by the regime.

Syrian Red Crescent workers "have shown a lot of dedication and determination and they are really doing a tremendous job", Dibeh Fakhr, a Red Cross spokeswoman said last month [February 2013] by telephone from Geneva. "We should not forget also that they are being killed. Seven volunteers have lost their life while on duty."

Last week, the UN undersecretary general for humanitarian affairs, Valerie Amos, acknowledged that the rebel-held north remained largely out of reach.

A "human tragedy is unfolding before our eyes," she said last month, according to Reuters. "We are crossing conflict lines, negotiating with armed groups on the ground, to reach more people in need. But we are not reaching enough of those who require our help."

"Limited access in the north is a major problem that we can only solve using alternative methods of aid delivery."

Ms. Amos said the Syrian government had recently authorized three additional international NGO's to work in Syria, raising the number authorized to 11.

The lack of aid reaching rebel-held areas has led to some calls for cross-border relief operations – but that also is problematic: The United Nations requires government permission from all parties involved, and the Syrian government has refused to allow UN convoys to cross from Turkey into northern Syria – where nearly all the border crossings are now under the control of the FSA.

Turkey has continued to maintain the official position that it will not violate Syrian sovereignty with cross-border operations. Nongovernmental agencies working in the region say that Turkey has nonetheless been the most permissive of Syria's neighbours in allowing aid to cross the border, despite its public stance. But Ankara's attitude has fluctuated after bombings at border crossings. Efforts by the Kurdistan Workers' Party, known by its Turkish acronym PKK, to take control of some areas along the northern border have also complicated the situation.

Despite the limitations on aid operations channelled through the UN's humanitarian networks, some nongovernmental organizations, including Médecins sans Frontières, have been working privately in rebel-held territory, and many have attested to the harsh conditions in those areas.

"This is exactly what we found. Liberated areas are getting virtually no aid from the UN or anyone else," said Kenan Rahmani, a board member of the Syrian American Council, the largest grassroots advocacy group for Syrians in the United States.

Earlier this year, Mr. Rahmani went into rebel-held regions where, he said, the group had been compiling a list of organizations trying to bring in aid.

"We definitely advocated very strongly for the US to use the Syrian opposition's coalition's Assistance Coordination Unit to distribute aid directly to liberated areas," said Mr. Rahmani, referring to a unit set up by the coalition at the request of the United Nations.

"The US has started doing that. Hopefully European governments will follow in that trend," he added.

Mr. Hossino, the Syrian-American analyst, said private organizations were increasingly able to enter the country with aid supplies; the problem for official aid flows were not primarily practical, he said. "This is about legal barriers."

After seeing the Azaz camp, Mr. Debeuf said he felt obliged to do something, even if it was outside the UN framework, to provide aid.

The main problem, he said, had been an absence of coordination between the European Union, the Syrian opposition coalition, the FSA, and the NGO's trying to distribute aid on the ground. So, he said, he had tried to bring those players together and push them toward greater cooperation.

"It isn't really my job, but there is no-one else to do it," he said.

Last month he organized a meeting in Turkey between a high-level delegation of European officials and two commanders of the FSA.

He was also instrumental in setting up this week's visit by General Idris to the European Parliament at the invitation of Guy Verhofstadt, the president of the ALDE group.

While many have criticized the Syrian opposition as being fractured and disorganized, General Idris said they have recently set up new structures needed for aid distribution. The general said all the documentation required is being gathered and can be provided by the FSA, including maps of where humanitarian and medical aid has been distributed and details of the recipients.

When the FSA fails to receive aid, he said, it causes them to lose support. "The aid is coming through the regime, and it isn't reaching us," he said. "People begin blaming us and we lose support."

Abu Eesa, a military commander in Manbij in northeast Aleppo, was one of two FSA generals to meet the delegation of high level European officials in Turkey in February. Mr. Eesa, who said he represented the more secular wings of the FSA, reinforced General Idris's warning.

"When I make promises on aid, I can't follow through," he said. "When Jabhat al-Nusra makes promises, they can follow through," he added, referring to the al-Nusra Front.

If Western governments continued to withhold aid supplies from the FSA command structures, he said, "All of Syria will turn to Jabhat al-Nusra, because they are providing this aid at the moment, and this is what people need."

Mr. Hossino, the political analyst said, "Everyone is trying to buy legitimacy in Aleppo and Idlib through aid. Aid is a weapon for all kinds of unsavoury actors, Jabhat al-Nusra, even the PKK. If the aid could get in, it could decrease this vacuum."

While legal obstacles to channelling aid through the UN system remain, and the concerns about aid falling into the wrong hands have not gone away, the pressure is growing for aid channels to be opened outside the framework of the United Nations. And with Secretary of State John Kerry of the United States recently pledging $60 million in additional non-lethal aid and training to the Syrian opposition, the pressure for Europe in particular to follow suit has been mounting.

"We need to take a leap of faith," Mr. Debeuf said. "Of course things will go wrong, but what we are doing now, is going very, very wrong, and we are only making two people stronger: Assad and Jabhat al-Nusra."

4. The Free Syrian Army does exist and is growing stronger by the day by Koert Debeuf & Response by Aron Lund

Published on *Syria Comment*, 19 March 2013

Syria Comment (*www.joshualandis.com*), the website of Joshua Landis, is one of the most widely visited online forums on Syria. Landis, who married a Syrian, is Associate Professor in the School of International and Area Studies at the University of Oklahoma and Director of the Center of Middle Eastern Studies. He is seen as one of the top experts on Syria. When Aron Lund, the editor of *Syria in Crisis*, an initiative of the Carnegie Center for International Peace, and the author of several reports and books on the Syrian opposition movement, posted a piece at Syria Comment[1] with the title "The FSA doesn't exist", I felt it essential to respond, as I had just returned from the headquarters of the FSA in Syria. Landis agreed to publish my response together with a counter-response from Lund. I thought it good to publish both as well. This piece has been spread and copied on other websites numerous times and gathered a lot of attention in Washington DC.

When I read Aron Lund's piece, "The FSA doesn't exist", I was utterly surprised. Of course the FSA exists. And it is changing rapidly. Over the past few months, the FSA has transformed itself from a loose structure into a functioning organization. In fact, what Lund describes is an era of the FSA that is over. It ignores the developments of the past several months and the present reality on the ground.

Last month, I visited Northern Syria three times with the Free Syrian Army (FSA). I spoke to many generals who had defected from the Syrian Army, to commanders on the ground, to people in the headquarters of the FSA and to military-civilian organizers of humanitarian aid from all parts of Syria. I also spent many hours with Dr. Brigadier General Salim Idriss, Chief of Staff of the FSA. I was in the middle of a battle at Quweris airport, then one of the main front lines.

Many of Lund's points were correct three months ago. But not now. Col. Riaad Al Assad (the first leader of the FSA) for example is completely

---

[1] View Lund's original article of 16 March 2013 on http://www.joshualandis.com/blog/the-free-syrian-army-doesnt-exist/

out of the picture, whatever he himself might say. Another example is Qasem Saadeddin. He did indeed try to create some unity in Homs and had difficulties in doing so. But that too is history. Today he is a commander of one of the five fronts under the umbrella of the FSA and he works closely with Idriss. It is also not true that Idriss would not use the 'brand' FSA. For example: he recently started his own Twitter and Facebook account, as well as one for FSA headquarters (@FSAHQ).

Nevertheless, I must admit that, at first sight, the structure of the FSA is utterly confusing. Whoever you talk to on the ground will pretend he is the most important commander in Syria. He will denounce formal structures and glorify his own past as a freedom fighter. I learned that the best strategy is smiling. And waiting. After an hour of ranting, the real story comes out. Every time. Then it emerges that the FSA does have a structure and that these commanders do operate within this structure, but that it is not fully established. The FSA is not just a brand. It does exist. The FSA building has a frame, but remains under construction.

The French Resistance

Aron Lund compares the FSA to the French Resistance in the Second World War. Spot on, I would say. But again, though his piece fits with the beginning of the French Resistance, the reality is that the FSA of today can be compared with the Free French Forces in a later, more organized stage.

The Free French Forces, established by Charles De Gaulle in London in 1940, was nothing more than a name and a few officers. One year later, small groups started to unite. However, it was still impossible to talk about a 'Free French Army'. There was not only a fragmentation in structure and command, but also in ideology. Call it the Riaad Al Assad era of the Free French Army.

It was only in May 1943 that (thanks to the work of Jean Moulin) the resistance forces were unified, militarily and politically, in the Conseil National de la Résistance (CNR) under the leadership of Charles De Gaulle. It took the Free French Forces three years to unite. After the unification, not all difficulties were gone. It took some time to become fully operative on the ground. Call it the Salim Idriss era.

The FSA Aron Lund is describing is the FSA of the Riaad Al Assad era, not the current one. At best, one could say his description lies somewhere in between the two, but it is certainly not describing today's reality.

The Riad Al Assad era or the former structure of the FSA

Up until a year ago, there was no structure at all in the Syrian armed rebellion. Every little group was called a battalion, whether it consisted of 20 or 200 fighters. The creation of the FSA by Col. Riad Al Assad in July 2011 was just as symbolic (and as important) as the creation of the Free French Forces by De Gaulle in 1940. On 23 October, the FSA merged with the Free Officers Movement, becoming the main organization for military defectors. Pure branding or not, it deserves the credit for at least trying to do something about the fragmentation. It gave the signal to the many battalion commanders that cooperation is the only way to go.

That is exactly what happened the next year. From July 2011 until September 2012, there were numerous initiatives to create larger entities. We saw the birth of brigades like Liwa Al Tawheed and Farouk[2]. We saw the creation of military councils, administrative councils, revolutionary councils and civilian councils. Some initiatives were pushed by the Friends of Syria or by individual countries. Aid, money or weapons were promised if the resistance would only get organized.

Unfortunately, these international actions lacked co-ordination as well. The result was that the Syrian opposition on the ground created several parallel structures. Another problem was the split between soldiers who had defected on the one hand and civilians who took up arms on the other. Defector-officers from the Syrian army organized themselves in military councils, while the civilians created revolutionary councils. In some places, like in Homs, there were even two military councils. Although these councils often co-operated in battles on the ground, the lack of unity created a clear disadvantage when it came drawing up a military strategy.

---

2   Liwa Al Tawheed or Tawheed Brigade is a brigade of more or less 10,000 Syrian rebels. It was founded in July 2012 and is mainly fighting in Aleppo. The Farouk Brigades are one of the largest units of the Free Syrian Army. It was founded in Homs in October 2011 and contains between 15,000 and 20,000 rebel fighters.

This lack of unity and strategy not only meant a disadvantage in the field, it also helped Assad's propaganda. Even as the FSA had no communication strategy at all, the Assad machine knew well what to do: discredit the FSA. There are three lines of attack:

1. The FSA is chaos. So it's Assad or chaos in Syria and the region.
2. The FSA is a danger to minorities. Assad is the only guarantee for the security of minorities in Syria.
3. The FSA is extremist. Assad is the only one who can keep out Al Qaeda.

I have been surprised to see how well organized the Assad communication machine is.

In every country in the West, media groups are spreading these three messages. Meanwhile, the FSA, which has too many self-appointed spokespersons (as Lund correctly spells out) and lacks a clear message on what it wants and who it is, is slowly losing the communications war.

The Salim Idriss era or the new structure of the FSA

On 7 December 2012, 260 officers of the FSA gathered in Antalya in Turkey. They elected a Higher Council of Revolutionary and Military Forces and a Chief of Staff, Dr. Brigadier General Salim Idriss. Idriss had defected in June 2012. The main reason he was elected was his talent for persuading people in a softly spoken way. He is more a Montgomery than a Patton. Col. Riad Al Assad wasn't present at the meeting. They decided he would keep the title of General Commander of the FSA, but this would be a symbolic rather than an operational title. His era is over.

In Antalya, the revolutionary and military components were merged. So, instead of military councils and revolutionary councils, there are now civilian-military councils. They also organized the FSA into five fronts: the Northern Front (Aleppo and Idlib), the Eastern Front (Raqqa-Deir Ezzor and Al Hassakah), the Western Front (Hama-Latakia-Tartus), the Central Front (Homs-Rastan) and the Southern Front (Damascus-Dar'a-Suwayda).

Each front has its civilian-military council and its commander. Each region/city within the front has its deputy commander, with its own civilian-military council. I met with two front commanders: Qasem

Saad Eddin, commander of the Central Front, and Abdelbasset Tawil, commander of the Northern Front, and with the latter's deputy commanders. They showed me detailed, strategic military plans. They also showed me lists of who received which weapons. It was clear that they were in close contact with Salim Idriss. Because of the strategic importance of Homs, Qasem Saad Eddin has an office next to that of Salim Idriss in the headquarters of the FSA. So Saadeddin is not a loose canon (anymore), as Lund has written.

The Higher Council of Revolutionary and Military Forces consists of 30 members. Every front has six representatives in the Council: three military and three civilian. They are mainly responsible for the search for and distribution of ammunition. Contrary to what has been promised, very few weapons are coming in. I saw how the FSA had to fight cluster bombs in Quweris with self-made arms.

Just like the Free French Forces did in 1943, Idriss has started creating a political line for the FSA. Until recently, we only knew what they were fighting against: Assad. Now they are trying to formulate what they are fighting for and get their spokesmen on the same page. The message in English and Arabic of Salim Idriss on the second anniversary of the Syrian revolution is an example of how they are moving forward on this.[3]

FSA is a bottom-up unification, still under construction

No one will deny that, while the FSA has taken big steps forward, there is still a long way to go to become a well-functioning, united force like the French resistance of 1943. Idriss has to unify battalions that are used to working independently. It takes a huge effort to convince them to walk in the same direction. What are the main problems?

1. There is hardly any communication infrastructure. Today, commanders have to communicate through Skype, yet in many places there is no Internet connection. Many officers have to travel to the headquarters to exchange information. It is very difficult to organize and unify an army in these conditions. That is why we should not be surprised if,

---

3   Message of FSA General Commander Salim Idriss of 15 March 2013, marking the second anniversary of the Syrian revolution, in which he states that the FSA is fighting to protect the Syrian people against the attacks by the Syrian government and for a free and democratic Syria for all Syrians. See www.youtube.com/watch?v=yEBHVCjxYQo.

at a certain moment, one of the battalions is acting on its own or is making a strategic mistake.
2. There are hardly any arms coming in. I was present for two days at the headquarters of the FSA. I saw officers coming from Homs, Deir Ezzor and many other places who wanted to meet with Chief of Staff, Salim Idriss, to get weapons. They were all pretty desperate. I heard many times: "How can we win the war, if we don't have arms against these planes or tanks?" A Chief of Staff only gets recognition and authority if he can arm his soldiers. This is basic. De Gaulle didn't unify because of his charisma alone.
3. Getting totally fragmented forces on the same page takes time. A number of the battalions, certainly the revolutionary ones, have no experience in fighting in a hierarchy. So, although they might recognize the authority of the Higher Military Council, they still don't always understand what exactly that means in the day-to-day battle. Give them some time.
4. The growing importance of extremist battalions like Jabhat Al Nusra is a problem for the image and the organization of the FSA. Lund writes that they do not use the brand of the FSA. Of course they don't – and they never will. They are not part of the FSA and never will be. The fact that the other groups do use the name of the FSA means they distance themselves from Nusra and its jihadist ideology.

The FSA deserves our support

It is fair to say that the FSA is not the well-oiled force some are dreaming of. But it is unfair and incorrect to say that the FSA does not exist and that it is not more than a brand.

We can't expect a bottom-up resistance to become a unified front in a few months (look at France during the Second World War). Becoming cynical or giving up on the FSA would be one of the biggest strategic mistakes the West could make.

Last month's work is done and a lot of progress has been made. If the international community decides to support the FSA, it will help them even more to unify, strategize and avoid mistakes. There is a structure of command. The headquarters will only provide arms to those battalions that follow their instructions. But they are still waiting for those arms. What *is* coming in is peanuts compared with what they need to win the war against one of the most brutal dictators in the world. What are we waiting for?

Aron Lund responds:

Koert Debeuf seems to have read my post a little carelessly. I did not deny the existence of (many) factions using the FSA name. Rather, I discussed the media's use of the FSA term, and stated that 'the FSA' does not exist, if understood as a single organization. The wording might have been a little provocative, but the fact itself should be uncontroversial for anyone who is following events in Syria.

There are undoubtedly many groups calling themselves FSA in Syria today, and indeed outside of Syria. They include both purported leaders and spokespersons, and fighting units on the ground. Some are closely linked to each other, and some work on their own. This reflects the way that the term is used as a synonym for 'the resistance' by many Syrians, and not necessarily to refer to a cohesive organization.

The problem I tried to address in my post is that different media organizations have been relying on several different 'FSA' spokespersons and leaders, few of whom represent any significant segment of fighters on the ground. They are routinely allowed to speak on behalf of the FSA (generally understood to make up most of the armed insurgency) without reporters making any attempt to define their real (and most often marginal) role within the insurgency. This has created an extreme lack of clarity in reporting, and it continues to confuse both regular newspaper readers and top officials.

When Debeuf complains that I haven't understood that Col. Riaad Al-Assad "is completely out of the picture, whatever he himself might say", then, to the contrary, that was exactly my point. Despite his complete lack of control over the armed insurgency, Col. Asaad is still routinely being interviewed by major news organizations as a commander of the FSA, misleading the general public into believing that his statements represent some significant portion of the armed movement in Syria. They do not.

Mea culpa

I will gladly admit that Debeuf makes some interesting arguments, and that he corrects a couple of faults of mine. His travels in northern Syria have put him in contact with a few of the most well-known rebel representatives and commanders. As an outside observer of events in Syria, I can't claim to have this kind of experience – I work with what I've got, and I'm always eager to hear from people who bring new facts to the table.

For example, I wasn't aware that Col. Qasem Saadeddine collaborates so closely with Salim Idriss, and I humbly stand corrected on that count.

Debeuf is also right that Salim Idriss and his General Staff now use the FSA term – despite the fact that the organization did not emerge under that name, and many of its member units have previously renounced the FSA label. In my defense, the Twitter account and other statements that Debeuf refers to had just been made when I wrote my post, and I wasn't aware of them at the time. But bottom line, he's right, and I was wrong.

Tua culpa

Even so, I believe Debeuf is far too optimistic in his view of the Salim Idriss network as a functioning nation-wide leadership, and that he has accepted too uncritically the explanations provided by his contacts in Syria. I've read Debeuf's original reports from Syria for the ALDE political group in the European Parliament. I note that he then presented the FSA as a neatly two-pronged structure of defected military and civilian revolutionary commanders. This seems wildly implausible, and contradicts most reporting from reporters and opposition members on the ground in Syria.

In his reports, Debeuf also claimed, on the subject of FSA organization, that one "Ahmed Abeit" has been "elected the general commander of all revolutionary structures for the whole of Syria". That was certainly news to me, and I imagine that it will be news to most Syrian revolutionaries as well. While I can't know for sure, it seems to be a reference to Ahmed Abeid, a rebel leader in Azaz. He might be a big guy around those parts, and among the rebels Debeuf traveled with, but he is certainly not the main internal commander of the Syrian insurgency.

What the Homsi said

Returning to Col. Qasem Saadeddine, Debeuf also notes that he is the General Staff's commander of the "Central Sector". That's certainly the official line, but how can such a claim be taken at face value?

The General Staff's Central Sector mainly includes Homs, formerly the main front of the uprising, which has been devastated by Assad's bombardment. The insurgency in this area is notoriously divided, not only due to the crippling government siege of Homs City, but also because of internal disagreements among the rebels.

Below is a list I recently compiled of factions currently active in Homs City and the surrounding countryside. It is far from exhaustive, and runs in no particular order. Note also that many, if not most, of these groups are themselves composed of semi-independent sub-factions:

Liwa Talbisa, Liwa Rijal Allah, Liwa Fajr al-Islam, Kataeb Ahl al-Athar (part of the Jabhat al-Asala wal-Tanmiya, a Salafi alliance), Katibat Shuhada Tal-Kalakh, Katibat Mouawiya lil-Maham al-Khassa, Liwa al-Quseir, several subunits of Kataeb al-Farouq, several other small Syria Liberation Front factions which are allied to Kataeb al-Farouq, al-Murabitoun (the armed wing of the Homs Revolutionaries' Union), Firqat al-Farouq al-Mustaqilla, Liwa al-Nasr, Katibat Thuwwar Baba Amr, Harakat al-Tahrir al-Wataniya, Jund al-Sham (Lebanese jihadis), armed groups affiliated to the Muslim Brotherhood (like Liwa Dar' Ahrar Homs, Liwa Dar' al-Haqq, and Liwa Dar' al-Hudoud), Jabhat al-Nosra, the Syrian Islamic Front (including the five Ahrar al-Sham factions Katibat Junoud al-Rahman, Katibat al-Hamra, Katibat Ansar al-Sunna wal-Sharia, Katibat Adnan Oqla, and Katibat Ibad Allah; and Liwa al-Haqq and its sub-factions, such as Katibat al-Ansar, Katibat al-Furati, etc)... and many others.

How does the FSA come into the picture? Sure, some of these groups use the FSA label to refer to themselves and their allies, but most do not. Some clearly receive arms through the Salim Idriss network, and some clearly do not. Some of the commanders in the Homs region have publicly declared their support for Salim Idriss, or allowed their representatives to be appointed to the General Staff's on-paper hierarchy – but others consider him a foreign-based usurper of revolutionary legitimacy.

We can quibble about how to classify these Homs factions, and what percentage could legitimately be subsumed under the 'FSA' label. But to imagine that Col. Qasem Saadeddine – or anyone else – exerts any real control over this sprawling mass of rebel factions is, frankly, delusional.

What this means for policy-makers

The fact of the matter is that the Syrian insurgency was always, and remains, deeply disorganized, despite persistent (and commendable) attempts by many Syrian opposition politicians and rebel commanders to form a joint leadership.

This is a tragedy, both for the opposition, and for Syria as a nation, but to recognize this fact is not, as Debeuf implies, a way to support the Syrian government. In fact, one can draw very different policy conclusions from the divided nature of the rebel movement.

One could argue that the lack of opposition unity speaks against arming the revolutionary movement, since there's no guarantee that weapons will be used effectively or stay in 'approved' rebel hands. But one could also legitimately argue that the only way to help midwife a central rebel leadership is by sponsoring a core network from abroad – to turn it into a 'magnetic pole' which will attract other factions. (This is what's now being done with Salim Idriss and the General Staff.) Both these positions are valid, in their own way, and merit careful consideration.

At the end of the day, however, I do believe that whatever side you're on in the Syrian conflict, and whatever political strategy you prefer to see implemented, good policy must be based on a careful examination of the available facts – not on political spin, rumours, or emotional arguments. Clearing up the extreme confusion surrounding the FSA term is only one of many steps to take, if a sensible Syria policy is ever to emerge.

5. What does the Free Syrian Army want?
Published on *Fikra Forum*, The Washington Institute, 28 March 2013

I have been to Northern Syria three times since January 2013 with a mission of exploring how the Free Syrian Army (FSA) functions. Before going to Syria, I had read many articles and seen many videos from citizen-journalists, but being on the ground, seeing things with my own eyes, made quite a difference.

I saw how two huge missiles from the Assad regime destroyed a marketplace in Azaz during its most crowded time and how all bakeries have been bombed. I slept in the houses of soldiers while hearing bombs being dropped from planes overhead. Two generals took me to the battle for Quweris airport, a major frontline, where I saw how the FSA fought with makeshift arms as the regime fired cluster bombs.

I also had the honour of being the first foreigner to visit the FSA headquarters. I met with many generals, commanders and soldiers from all over Syria in order to understand what they stand for. And I had many talks with Salim Idriss, the newly elected chief of staff of the FSA, whose visit to the European Parliament on 6 March 2013 I organised.

An image that doesn't fit with reality

Every conversation I had with FSA commanders started with the same two questions: "Why is the West not supporting us?" followed by "Are we the terrorists you thought we were?" Without waiting for the answer, each tried to explain that they are not looking for sectarian violence. I heard countless stories of their efforts to protect Christians against attacks from the regime. I also sat with a Christian FSA general who only identified himself as Christian when I started to discuss the issue.

Every story came down to the same four points:

1. We do not want an Islamic state – freedom and democracy is for all Syrians, regardless of their religion or ethnicity.

2. The jihadis are not part of the FSA; however, they are well trained, well organized, and they have arms and money. Unlike the FSA, brigades like Jabhat al-Nusra are able to pay their soldiers $200 per month. That's what is making them stronger every day.
3. We are here to protect the people, schools, and hospitals, to organize aid, and to help the refugees. We try to organize police forces and courts, but the constant and random shelling makes this process extremely difficult. On top of that, almost all humanitarian aid goes through Assad and the Red Crescent and does not reach the rebel areas.
4. We do not have the right weapons to fight against planes, tanks and ground-to-ground missiles. The arms which do come in are always too light and are sometimes completely useless.

I must say that everything I saw during my trips confirms their stories. Their biggest frustration is that this is completely unknown outside Syria. What we see of the FSA is very confusing, an image that is fuelled by Assad's propaganda. One of the regime's methods is to systematically spread jihadi videos every time the FSA wins ground or captures an important strategic point. This way, the outside world gets the idea that it is not the FSA, but Jabhat al-Nusra that is succeeding militarily.

The new structure of the FSA

On 6 December 2013, more than 250 officers of the FSA gathered in Antalya, Turkey. There they elected Salim Idriss to the role of chief of staff and 30 officers into the Higher Revolutionary Military Council. They also organized the FSA into five fronts, each with its own commander who cooperates closely with the chief of staff: the Northern Front (Aleppo, Idlib), the Eastern Front (Raqqa, Deir al-Zour, al-Hasaka), the Western Front (Hama, Latakia, Tartus), the Central Front (Homs, Rastan), and the Southern Front (Damascus, Dara, Swaydda)[1].

The new structure strengthens the organization because it unites the military and the revolutionary forces under one command. However, the organization is still new, and is therefore rather weak while under

---

[1] As discussed previously in '3. The Free Syrian Army does exist and is growing stronger by the day' (19 March 2013).

construction. Many fighters and battalions have never fought in a regular army and must still learn to follow a common strategy and code of conduct.

Here we come to the question of the chicken and the egg. The West expects the FSA to be properly organized before they will give them equipment and arms, but the FSA is having a hard time becoming properly organized as they lack basic equipment like satellite phones. They lack the money to pay hungry soldiers and they have not even enough arms to give every fighter a weapon. Only one in two people – perhaps fewer – who want to fight have a gun. This is one of the main reasons that more soldiers of the Syrian military are not defecting.

The West is creating a new enemy

It is common knowledge that Assad is still receiving arms from Russia and Iran. Observers assume that the FSA too is being armed in some way or another. But this is not what I have seen on the ground, and this prevalence of assumptions and wrong portrayals is hugely frustrating for the FSA commanders. Many are convinced that, while the West is saying they want Assad to go, they in fact want him to stay. The FSA still sees the West as their ideological allies in their fight against a brutal dictatorship; therefore, they cannot understand why no help is forthcoming.

If asked what exactly the FSA wants from the West, the answer is pretty clear: all help is needed. They need anti-aircraft weapons to stop the planes, weapons to stop the tanks and the missiles, and technical equipment. And when I asked what they thought about a no-fly zone, their answer was: That would be wonderful. It would stop the destruction and the killing of citizens.

The conclusion is simple: failing to make the FSA stronger is instead strengthening Assad and the jihadists. This is a choice between a democratic Syria, a dictatorship, and an Islamic state, for we are now either building a Syria that will be in favour of the West, or we are creating a new enemy.

6. Not the jihadists but we are the problem
Published on *EU Observer*, 28 April 2013

A few days ago, a Belgian woman called to ask if I could contact the Syrian jihadists of Jabhat Al Nusra. Her son left his family to join them a month and a half ago and since then she hasn't heard anything from him. I had to disappoint her, as I have no contact with the jihadists. In fact, when in Syria, I always try to avoid them.

She was of course very worried, but also embarrassed. Her son is fighting in a battle she does not at all support, nor even understand. I kind of recognize this embarrassment as it made me recall the story of a relative whom my family hardly ever talks about. He was killed in the Second World War when he decided to fight with the Nazis 'against the Communists'. He believed he had to choose between Rome and Moscow, between God and the Devil and that this choice needed sacrifice even if it meant his own life.

Each time I travelled to Syria over the past months, I saw jihadists taking the same plane and the same bus as I did and following the same illegal way to enter northern Syria. What drew my attention and worried me each time was the self-confidence in their eyes, the acceptance that they would die in Syria. Above all, they were proud of it. The jihadists know they are going to be at the front line of the battle and that some people will admire them for that. And for them, this is exactly what they have missed in their lives: admiration, guidance and heroic acts.

What disturbed me most, however, wasn't seeing these jihadists entering Syria. I can't stop them anyway. No, what is worse is that I didn't see anyone else entering Syria. No relief teams, no doctors and no trucks loaded with aid for the other Syrians, for the vast majority of the rebels who have nothing to do with the jihadists' ideologies. While Al Qaeda's friends possess weapons and money to distribute to their fighters, people are dying of hunger in refugee camps supervised by the FSA.

We in the West are so mesmerized by a small group of radicals that we have lost the ability to see the reality. Fearing the ghost of Afghanistan, we decided to do nothing. Because if we do nothing, we can't do anything, wrong. We are committing a huge mistake. Because by doing nothing we only make Assad and the jihadists stronger, while we leave those who share our values on their own.

The main excuse I hear for not intervening is: we don't know what the Free Syrian Army is and we don't know what they want. It's a silly excuse. Because if you don't know, it's simply because you haven't made the effort to know. It's not that difficult. Two weeks ago, I had a dinner in Turkey with the Chief of Staff of the FSA, Salim Idriss, and four of the five Front Commanders. Anyone who makes the effort to go to Antakya will be able to meet any officer of the FSA. You will hear that they want freedom and democracy, that they try everything to respect human rights, protect the minorities and help the refugees. But you will also hear that they don't have the means to achieve these goals properly.

Anyone who makes an effort can reach the refugee camps in Syria easily and will be able to see how disastrous and inhuman the situation is there; how children spend sometimes days without food or even weeks without milk; how they die because of injuries, caused by a shrapnel, due to lack of medical care. You will then see that our aid to Syria is mainly distributed through Assad, which is why almost no aid is reaching the 'liberated areas'. Whoever makes an effort will see that it is the soldiers of Assad, and no one else, that are attacking and bombarding civilians.

But, apparently all this requires too much effort. We prefer to do nothing "as we don't know what will happen after Assad falls". Just imagine that the Americans and the British hadn't entered in WWII because of fear of communists, and because they too didn't know "what would happen after Hitler falls".

Should we be surprised then that those who fight for a better Syria are getting more and more angry and frustrated with the West? In their eyes, the only thing that comes from the West is jihadist fighters – however small and insignificant their numbers – while the secular forces and the Syrian people are being left to their own devices.

It is of course justified to feel uncomfortable and even fearful for 'our boys' who go to this far and unknown Syria to fight for the sake of forming an Islamic State. However, we will not solve this problem by trying to stop our 'boys' from going. We will only solve the crisis if we start to engage with Syria itself. It's less difficult than we might think. We just need to make the effort.

7. We never learn: Syrian lessons from Bosnia
Posted on The German Marshall Fund of the United States, 10 June 2013

Srebrenica, 26 May 2013. I am staring at almost 8,000 tombstones. Males between 12 and 80 years old have been massacred because they believed in the wrong God. It all happened in a few days. We all know the story of Srebrenica, but when you stand in the middle of the graveyard, it feels like you're smashed against a huge wall. The wall of genocide, of crimes against humanity. And you think: *never again*. I had exactly the same feeling in Auschwitz and Rwanda: *never again*. But that's a wish rather than a reality. Because in the real world, it does happen over and over again.

I travelled to Srebrenica as part of GMF's Transatlantic Leadership Seminar. Back in Sarajevo, the group I travelled with had had a chance to learn more about the Bosnian war. My jaw dropped. As I work a lot on Syria and Libya, I often couldn't believe what I was hearing. In a nutshell: Bosnia-Herzegovina is a former Ottoman province with a multi-ethnic population. In the 1991 census, 44% of the population considered themselves Muslim, now Bosniak (mostly Sunni); 32.5% Serb (Orthodox); and 17% Croat (Catholic), with 6% describing themselves as Yugoslav (Jewish, Roma, and other). During the break-up of the former Yugoslavia, Bosnia-Herzegovina declared itself independent in April 1992. A part of the Serbian population living predominantly in the north and east of Bosnia rejected independence and declared their own state: *Republika Serpska*.

The start and the end of the war in Bosnia

Many are convinced that the war started when Serbia's President Slobodan Milosevic and Croatia's President Franjo Tudjman decided to partition Bosnia-Herzegovina between their two newly independent states. But the war didn't start just like that. Although there were some incidents, sectarian violence was not spontaneous, but provoked. Militias comprised of extremists and convicts were created to raid mixed villages and produce a sectarian war.

The Yugoslav National Army remained in the hands of the Serbs, while Croats quickly formed their own armed forces with the help of Croatia proper. When the bombing of Sarajevo and sectarian violence in Herzegovina began, the Bosniaks had virtually no arms with which to defend themselves. On top of that, the UN Security Council imposed an arms embargo, forcing the Bosniaks to rely only on arms they were able to make, smuggle, or seize from the enemy. There were many massacres of defenseless communities. All in all, around 100,000 people were killed, of which almost 70 percent were Bosniaks.

So how did the war end? After years of debate on lifting the arms embargo, the US decided to intervene. In the spring of 1994, it brokered a peace settlement between the Bosnian Croats and Muslim Bosniaks and, in the summer 1995, it led NATO to install a no-fly zone and use airstrikes to force the Bosnian Serbs to the negotiating table. On 21 November 1995, the Dayton Peace Agreement was signed.

And now Libya and Syria

It is very clear that without the no-fly zone in Libya, Benghazi would have been Sarajevo and Srebrenica combined. Gaddafi's troops were already entering the city when the first F-16s crossed the Libyan border.

Much more striking are the similarities between Bosnia and Syria. President Assad uses his Shabiha militias to massacre and to incite sectarian violence. In Syria there has never really been sectarian tension. This remains true even today, no matter what propaganda wants us to believe. Just like in Bosnia, there is an arms embargo preventing communities from defending themselves. Those arms the newly formed defense groups do have are improvised, smuggled, or appropriated from the army. But they are largely powerless against airstrikes and long-distance missiles that are destroying cities and killing tens of thousands of people.

For endangered communities in Bosnia, the situation was clear: genocide was being perpetrated against them. But for the international community, it all looked too messy and difficult to understand. The quick agreement after the intervention proved that, in the end, things were less difficult then they had appeared to be. I don't see much difference in Syria today. The question is: are we going to intervene, or will we never learn?

8. Syria: the land of broken promises
Published on *EU Observer*, 28 October 2013

"Yesterday the regime killed three of my close family members. They were in prison since one year (sic). Now they were killed on the same day." Salim Idriss, General Commander of the FSA, looked at me with glazed eyes. We met at the end of October, at the same place where he was holding talks with some of the rebel groups of the Syrian Islamic Army. This new coalition of some 50 rebel groups in Syria was formed on 29 September 2013. A few days before the official announcement, they had already declared they did not recognize the Syrian National Coalition and that they wanted Islamic law as the basis for legislation.

"If they are strong, why would they decide to talk to the official FSA almost immediately after their foundation?" I asked. The answer Idriss gave me was surprisingly obvious: they want more weapons and more money. The main group of the Islamic Army, Liwa al Islam, is part of the Supreme Military Council of the FSA (SMC). And they, like other groups of this Islamic Army, are represented in the SMC. Looking at the timing of the formation is what gives us the most insight into this development: two weeks after the US decision not to attack the Syrian army but make a deal with Russia to remove Assad's chemical weapons instead.

The frustration runs deep in the rebel camp. On the one side, they see extremist groups like the Al Qaeda linked Jabhat Al Nusra and ISIS (Islamic State of Iraq and Al Shams, an even more radical jihadist group that is being opposed by all other rebel groups) becoming stronger, better equipped and richer[1], while on the other side, the promised arms and other support to the FSA by the West is nothing more than a joke. A few days before the US attack that never happened, Secretary of State John Kerry called Idriss to guarantee the attack would happen. Indeed, it would have changed so much. The Syrian Army was frightened to death at the thought of the attack, while the ISIS was moving their headquarters every

---

[1] It is not clear who exactly is funding these extremist groups, but it is widely assumed that the source is private donors in Kuwait, Saudi Arabia, Qatar and the United Arab Emirates.

day, as they too were convinced they were to be bombed. It would have triggered a wave of defections. As a matter of fact, the wave had already started, with former Syrian Minister of Defence Ali Habib being the most symbolic.

The result of the non-attack was immediately clear. Bashar Al-Assad appeared on Fox news as if he had already won the war. And ISIS launched an attack on the strategically important city of Azaaz. Azaaz lies on the border with Turkey, controlling the way from Aleppo to Gaziantep. It is a stronghold of one of the FSA brigades, the Northern Storm, whom I met the first time I went into Syria. It must be said that this group does not consist of the most educated fighters and that they were not managing the liberated city as they should. They were also the ones who kidnapped the nine Lebanese pilgrims that were liberated last week[2]. So when ISIS attacked Azaaz, it believed it would be welcomed as liberators of the people from the Northern Storm 'crooks'. Not so. Strong groups such as Liwa Al Tawheed and Ahrar Al Shams came to stop ISIS, while the citizens of Azaaz started protesting against the presence of ISIS and the totalitarian rules it was imposing.

Six months earlier, in March 2013, I had spent a few days at the headquarters of the FSA[3]. It was just before ISIS was founded. I witnessed how, from the early morning until after midnight, FSA groups from all over Syria visited Salim Idriss. They all came with the same story: we can make progress but we need the right weapons. But instead of arms, President Obama decided to send hot meals. Again: ISIS did not exist at this stage and Jabhat Al Nusra didn't represent more than five percent of total rebel fighters. With proper arms, the FSA would not only have saved many lives, but the growth of these jihadist groups would also have been made impossible.

But here we are today, overseeing the mess we allowed to happen and wondering what we should do. Trying to forget our broken promises, we found a new one: Geneva II. Now, every Western country repeats that "the only way out for Syria is a political solution". The vast majority of the Syrians couldn't agree more. But how on earth is this going to happen now? The West has been defeated on the Russian diplomatic chessboard. After the chemical weapons deal, Assad feels victorious. Most of the

---

2   In May 2012, 11 Shia Lebanese pilgrims were kidnapped on their way back from Iran. Two of them were released quickly, but the 9 remaining hostages were set free in October 2012.
3   See '4. What does the Free Syrian Army want?' (28 March 2013).

world's attention is now going to the so-called terrorists and is hardly reporting his atrocities anymore. Assad is more than happy for us to try and find a political solution on the same chessboard he and his Russian friends played on – and won on – in the last game.

At the same time, there are serious cracks in the anti-Assad coalition. The new Egyptian government pulled out for internal reasons[4] and made a common stance of the Arab League as good as impossible... The Saudis were appalled by the sudden American-Russian deal, the non-attack and the rapprochement to Iran, but also angered by the fact that the US failed to inform the Kingdom about these crucial steps.

It is no coincidence that Saudi Arabia is behind the formation of the Islamic Army. Even though the new president of the Syrian Opposition Coalition (SOC) was a Saudi choice, it seems that Saudi Arabia has stopped its support for the SOC and is concentrating its efforts on the groups fighting on the ground. The statement of the Islamic Army of 24 September makes three things clear: first, no more support for the SOC; second, by asking for sharia, but excluding ISIS and Jabhat Al Nusra, the Islamic Army is clearly meant as a counterforce against these two Jihadi groups; third, as the main brigades of the army are part of the SMC, it is meant as a wake-up call for the FSA.

Last week in Gaziantep, I had a coffee with Mansour, an activist who spent one year in one of the worst prisons of the Syrian Air Force. From a secular family, he told me that one of his nephews had joined Jabhat Al Nusra. Not because he believed in jihad, but because he needed the money to buy food for his family. The big difference between Al Nusra and ISIS is that while all of the ISIS fighters are extremist jihadists, a lot of the Al Nusra fighters are not. They join Al Nusra because they need the money. FSA brigades don't pay, as they have no money. I heard this story time and again, inside and outside Syria. This is the reason why Jabhat Al Nusra and ISIS split after a short period of joining forces. Most Al Nusra fighters couldn't live with the 'extremist ISIS' way of working. Also, ISIS is seen as non-Syrian and most of the foreign fighters are with them.

What should be done? If we put all the pieces together, we must conclude that the situation is not that much different as it was six months ago. There is a military stalemate on the ground. The political opposition

---

4   President Morsi called for a jihad against the Syrian regime. After his removal on 3 July 2013, the new government took the opposite stance refusing to back the Syrian opposition and rebels. Egypt also started to deport Syrian refugees. See '17. How President Morsi ousted himself: a too short overview' (25 July 2013)

is divided. The Syrian army is not very strong and avoids fighting on the ground. Instead, they are targeting the population by bombing from the air and using long-distance missiles. Six months ago we feared Jabhat Al Nusra, today we fear ISIS. And, just like six months ago, Bashar Al Assad is not prepared to budge even an inch. Probably the only thing that has changed is the world's perception of the Syrian conflict. The propaganda machine of Assad has done a good job[5].

So, if we are serious about ending this catastrophic conflict, stopping the jihadists and ousting the most brutal dictator of the 21st century, there are limited options. A political solution will only be possible if the people around Assad – military or civilian – realise they can't win anymore. They will need to be convinced they have a better future without Assad. But as long as Assad remains in his 'winning mood', this will never happen. Therefore there is no other solution than to go back to square one: arm the FSA with weapons that can stop airplanes and long-distance missiles. Give them money so they can pay their soldiers. Give them training so they stop committing war crimes and punish those who do. Make sure that humanitarian aid is reaching all Syrians, including those in liberated and disputed areas. Because only a stronger FSA will be able to unite forces and negotiate the much-needed political solution for Syria.

---

[5] See '3. The Free Syrian Army does exist and is growing stronger by the day' (19 March 2013)

9. Assad is the problem, not the solution
Published on *EU Observer*, 21 January 2014

For the first time since the start of the Syrian revolution, both representatives of the opposition and the government would sit around the same table in order to find a way out of the crisis. This meeting, called Geneva II, started on 22 January 2014 and ended on 31 January. As expected, it was a meeting that generated a lot of frustration as no progress whatsoever has been made. The day before the conference, UN secretary general Ban Ki Moon announced that he invited Iran to be present at the meeting and that Iran accepted this invitation. The Syrian Opposition Coalition was furious and canceled its participation via Twitter. The United States then said that Iran could only attend if it accepted "a transition government of both members of the opposition and the regime" as agreed on the first Geneva conference of 30 June 2012. Iran refused and thus declined the invitation. The Syrian Opposition Coalition then announced that it would participate.

Tomorrow, 22 January 2014, the Geneva II Conference on Syria begins. After some deplorable miscommunication regarding the invitation of Iran, all of the main actors decided to participate. The aim of the conference is to find a way to end the devastating war in Syria. Up until a few weeks ago, the main issue on the table was how to build a transition government towards elections and whether or not Bashar Al Assad could be part of it. The paradigm has since changed into how the world can get rid of the Al Qaeda linked jihadists of ISIS, the Islamic State of Iraq and the Levant (Sham in Arabic).

However, the most surprising shift of the past weeks is the fact that Assad is back in the game. More and more people start to wonder if there is any alternative to Assad to fight jihadism in Syria. Didn't he always warn the world of the dangers of Al Qaeda if his regime should fall? The Assad regime might be bad, but a Caliphate under the leadership of the emir of ISIS is – no doubt – a far worse nightmare. Aren't Assad and his forces the only guarantee against a full-fledged sectarian war expanding over the entire region? And didn't Assad fulfil his promise and fully cooperate in destroying his chemical weapons? That at least seems to be the conviction of some European intelligence agencies, who have, apparently, already started to share information on jihadist forces with the intelligence services of Damascus.

By accepting Bashar Al Assad back into the fold we tend to distract from what has really been happening in Syria since the revolution broke out on 15 March 2011[1]. Even though there were no armed rebels during the first months of the revolt, Assad kept on repeating that the protesters were nothing more than terrorists and extremists. He must have been very happy when, in January 2012, the first jihadist group, Jabhat Al Nusra, finally appeared. He could use them as the reason for bombing Baba Amr (Homs) to the ground in February 2012 and (falsely) blame them for having perpetrated the massacre of Houla (Homs) in May of the same year.

The Assad regime must have been even happier when ISIS appeared as a force in Syria in April 2013. Now Assad could accuse them of his chemical attack in Ghouta in August 2013. With the help of Moscow, many even believed it. It was this doubt that made the US and the UK change their mind about attacking Syria and instead support Russia's proposal to destroy Syria's chemical weapons (a scapegoat). Suddenly, Assad became someone we can make deals with, while the rebel forces and the political opposition remained divided and inefficient.

But even if we assume that ISIS and Al Qaeda are behind all these crimes against humanity, we should ask ourselves: why is Assad not fighting harder against them? Instead of throwing barrel bombs on neighbourhoods in Aleppo, he could attack Raqqa, the stronghold of ISIS. But he doesn't. Instead of employing a large amount of soldiers to starve out 20,000 Palestinian refugees in Yarmouk, he could use these troops to fight jihadists in the province of Deir Ezzor. But he doesn't.

It is not Assad, but a coalition of rebel groups and the Free Syrian Army that decided to fight against ISIS and liberate towns and cities from their reign of terror. It is not Assad, but the inhabitants of these towns who started to revolt against the rule of Al Qaeda. Syrian citizens and Syrian rebel groups are the ones taking a stance against the foreign fighters of ISIS, not Assad. It is remarkable to note that ISIS has used many more suicide attacks against the coalition of rebel forces than it has against the regime.

---

1   See '1. Syria is a second Bosnia. Assad is Milosevic' (29 May 2012)

In the search for a solution, it is clear that dismissing everyone connected to the current regime would be a severe mistake. People of the current administration and army are absolutely crucial to create the necessary stability and to rebuild the country. But thinking we should keep Bashar Al Assad in place as a partner against Al Qaeda and other affiliated jihadist groups would be an error that would go down in the country's history. This scenario is unacceptable to at least half of the Syrians. It would also be a signal to all dictators that the more innocent citizens you kill, the more sectarian violence you instigate and the more extremism you accept, the more chances you have the world will forgive you.

There should be no misunderstanding: keeping Bashar Al Assad in place is the best guarantee that the war, the slaughter, the starvation and the torture will continue for many years to come. It will further expand the conflict throughout the region and will increase the number of refugees worldwide. They will not return if the reason for their misery stays put. A so-called leader who bombs his own people with SCUD rockets is no leader and never will be.

LIBYA
Reflections from October to May 2013

Libya is an excellent example of how the West can help to change things for the best *and* for the worst. In Libya, the best thing the West (France in particular) has done is to intervene at the right moment. Without intervention, Benghazi would without doubt have turned into a massacre of horrifying proportions. The Libyan revolution started in Benghazi and Gaddafi was determined to exterminate the revolutionaries there to the last man. Intervening was simply the only action the world could take.

Unfortunately, once the Gaddafi regime had fallen, Western support vanished. Even though the Libyans kept asking for help in organizing their security forces, in facilitating dialogue and for supporting democracy, our door was kept closed. Some support did come from the West, but overall, it was too little and too late.

I visited Libya three times. The first time (March 2012), I was asked by the newly founded National Forces Alliance to help them create a party structure, a programme and a campaign. The second time (November 2012), I organized a one-week training for the 39 elected Members of Parliament on how politics work. The third visit (March 2013), in which I was accompanying a delegation of ALDE, was to celebrate the one-year anniversary of the National Forces Alliance.

Each time, it was clear that the Libyans (contrary to the Egyptians) were eager to learn and to take advice on how to do a better job in politics. If it had been possible, they would have insisted I stay in Tripoli and bring in as many advisors as possible. I don't know why, but for some reason the Libyans seem to care more about the future of their country than about their own political careers. Cynics would say this is because they've never known what a political career is, as Gaddafi forbade organizations of any nature whatsoever.

Libya has a good chance at success. They have only about 3.5 million inhabitants and enormous reserves of oil. All they need is an agreement on how to distribute the wealth in a way everybody is happy. With a well-organized national dialogue, Libya could become a model state within a few years.

This might sound overly optimistic in the light of what is happening there each day: assassinations, bomb attacks, kidnappings, militias fighting, parliamentary decisions taken under threats of those same militias, and so forth. But I remain convinced that, with proportionate support from the European Union, Libya can take some important steps forward. That is the message I was trying to offer in my pieces on Libya, as well as in many press releases sent out by the ALDE in the past three years.

1. *Zenga Zenga* Democracy
Published on *EU Observer*, 23 October 2011

During one sleepless night, surfing Youtube, I found a film of a disco in Tunis in which people were dancing to the so-called 'Gaddafi song'. It is a great mix of the mad speech Muammar Gaddafi gave some months ago to warn the Libyan opposition that he would hunt them down wherever they went: "*Dar, dar, beit, beit, zenga, zenga*"... ("house by house, apartment by apartment, alleyway by alleyway").

In the past two months, the roles were reversed. The rebels hunted Gaddafi *dar, dar, beit, beit, zenga, zenga*.

Last Thursday, 20 October, they found him in Sirte, in a pipe. When some rebels dragged him out, he asked one: "What have I done wrong to you?" The guy must have been too baffled to answer this appalling question. What have you done wrong to me? Um, well, where to begin? The last words of one of the cruellest dictators of our times tell us a lot about how this madman's mind functioned. He probably really thought that murdering, torturing, raping and starving people was for the best of his country.

But now that the dust is settling, the biggest challenge for Libya is about to begin: the building of a new country on the ruins of the old one. More than 40 years of leadership under the *frère guide*, the King of Kings of Africa, the leader of the revolution, have left a country without political parties, without intellectuals, without trade unions, without political structures and without civil society. Libya is a political desert.

Luckily, there are wise and strong people like Mahmoud Gebril around. Without trying to be politically biased, the ALDE group can be proud of the fact they were the first to invite Gebril to Europe, the first to recognise the Transitional National Council (the Libyan rebel government) and to support its demand for a no-fly zone.

But a few strong people is not enough. An entire new political structure has to be built. No wonder that even as NATO gets out of Libya, a new Western army comes in: the army of democracy builders. They will give all possible support to constructing a parliamentary democracy, based on models in the West.

At this point, we must be brave and dare to ask if trying to export our own parliamentary system is really the best thing to do.

It is a question all the more urgent as our system is currently facing its own problems. Nobody can deny we have problems of legitimacy, problems of inability to give proper answers to the financial and economic crisis. Thousands of *indignados* are filling the streets of our capitals. In short, we must dare to admit that our system of democracy needs some rethinking.

So instead of trying to introduce our rules of politics in Libya, would it not be more effective to use the Libyan political desert to create a new democratic oasis? A system with more citizen participation, more involvement of people in the decision-making process, a stakeholder democracy, a system in which the "heart of power really is empty", as the French philosopher Claude Lefort put it.

Instead of lagging behind, Libya could become a model of a new kind of democracy. There are some sharp-thinking Libyans who want to experiment and to give the people in the street the opportunity to co-build a new country. Let us think, together with them, how to build a *zenga zenga* democracy.

2. The untold story of Libya's Mahmud Gebril
Published on *EU Observer*, 18 May 2013

This piece has been translated into Arabic and published on several Libyan websites. It was written as a defense of Mahmud Gebril, who was under attack in the Libyan (Muslim Brotherhood) media, who were intent on spreading the idea that his share in convincing the West to intervene was negligible. Gebril was also being criticized for the fact that he went to the ALDE group in the European Parliament. Libyan media even went so far as to spread pictures of Gebril, Guy Verhofstadt and myself together, saying that he was connected to liberal politicians who support gay rights. On top of the accusations, Mahmud Gebril was the prime victim of the Political Isolation Law, that excluded all politicians and officials that had worked in one way or another with the Gaddafi regime.

One of these days, Libyan Members of Parliament, Ministers and most probably even the President of the GNC (General National Congress) will have to resign, due to the Political Isolation Law. After this law was voted in by the Libyan parliament, I wrote on Twitter: "Mahmud Gebril is excluded from running in elections. The man who prevented the Benghazi massacre. Justice?" I was pretty surprised by the reactions I received. And not necessarily by the least informed. They all found my statement very much exaggerated. The fact that Gebril was on TV a lot did not automatically mean he had done something substantial, they said. It made me realize that the real story behind the no-fly zone in Libya has not been told.

The most repeated version of what happened has been loudly spread by Bernard Henri-Lévy: how he went to Libya, came back to Paris and convinced Sarkozy to plea for a no-fly-zone. It was also BHL who convinced Mahmud Gebril to come to Paris and it was he who pushed the president to recognize the National Transition Council. The very short version of the heroic story of Henri-Lévy is most probably true. Sarkozy was the first one to call for a no-fly zone in Libya, just one week after the revolution started on February 17, 2011. I do not doubt BHL did play his role in this decision. But in the rest of this history, the starring role was not BHL, but Mahmud Gebril.

In the first week of March, a Libyan opposition member in Brussels called Louis Michel to ask if Michel would meet with members of the National Transition Council. Michel is the former Foreign Minister of Belgium and now a Member of European Parliament. The first thing Michel did was to call Guy Verhofstadt, former Prime Minister of Belgium and currently president of the Alliance of Liberals and Democrats in the European Parliament (ALDE). They both agreed they should invite these Libyan opposition leaders to the ALDE Group in the European Parliament in Strasbourg.

Getting the Libyans to Strasbourg was not easy. The meeting of the ALDE group was scheduled on 8 March, but we could only start with the visa procedure for the Libyans on 5 March. I called the Chief of Staff of the Foreign Minister of Belgium. Apart from the fact that he was not very cooperative (who were these Libyan rebels?), he explained that an emergency visa procedure does exist, but is only valid in the country that issues it and not for the entire Schengen zone. So, we had to call the French government. My colleague got permission and the relevant security clearance from the French Minister of Interior. A former advisor of President Sarkozy, he of course warned the President that two members of the NTC would be in France: Dr. Mahmud Gebril and Dr. Ali A.S. Al-Issawi.

The only thing we knew about the gentlemen was that Al-Issawi was the Libyan ambassador in India and that he had defected to the opposition in February as a reaction to Muamar Gaddafi's violent response to the revolution. Of Mahmud Gebril we knew next to nothing. The contact person we had to call for the more practical arrangements was a lawyer living in Geneva. His name was Ali Zeidan. I only realized much later that this person is in fact the Libyan Prime Minister today.

At the meeting of the ALDE group (which was open to other parties as well) on 8 March, Mahmud Gebril surprised everyone. This unknown man was so brief and precise in his description of the situation of the Libyan revolution – and in his demands to the European Union – that it was almost impossible not to be convinced. Gebril spoke with authority. Most of all, he made clear to everyone that there would be a serious alternative if Gaddafi fell.

Gebril asked three things of the international community:

1. Recognition of the National Transitional Council as the legitimate representative of the Libyan people;
2. Guarantee the supply of humanitarian assistance to the Libyan people, particularly where there is shortage of food and medicine and a lack of secure telephone lines;
3. Enforce a no-fly zone (but no military intervention) to prevent further killing.

Guy Verhofstadt asked me to write these demands down in a press release, together with a plea to the international community to support each one.

We also tried to convince EU High Representative Cathy Ashton to meet with Gebril. She hesitated. A few days earlier she had received a common letter from all European ambassadors in Tripoli in which they stated it would be best for the EU not to take sides in the conflict. After all, what would the EU do if Gaddafi won? But a few hours later, her spokesperson told me at a coffee bar that she would meet him, but that it would be a secret meeting. The meeting apparently went well as he called to say it was okay for the press to know about it.

During the debate in the plenary of the European Parliament the next day, Ashton refused to promise anything regarding the possible recognition of the NTC, even though most speakers asked for this. I even had to go to her with a compromise proposal in which she would promise to put it on the table of the European Council. But as Ashton never moves without having consulted with the other Ministers of Foreign Affairs, she refused even to promise that.

President Sarkozy, on the contrary, did not hesitate. Originally, the plan of the Libyan delegation had been to go to Geneva after the plenary debate in Strasbourg. Zeidan knew his way around and would organize some interesting meetings. But the plans changed when the Elysée called them: the president of France wanted to meet them. Sarkozy knew he hadn't made a very good impression by not supporting the revolution in Tunisia back in 2010. Furthermore, he was not doing well in the opinion polls for the presidential elections to be held a few months later. He knew from his Interior Minister that the Libyan opposition was in the country and had probably seen the ALDE press release and he saw his chance. So, on 10 March that's where the delegation went.

I was driving home when I heard on the news that Sarkozy had recognized the National Transition Council and, of course, supported Gebril's other two demands (Sarkozy had called for a no-fly zone before).

Nobody in the French government had been informed. Not even his foreign minister Alain Juppé. Juppé and his German colleague, Guido Westerwelle, had just closed their bilateral meeting and were walking towards the press point, when one of Juppé's advisors gave him a small piece of paper. To his surprise, he read that his president had just recognized the NTC. Although not known for hesitating, Sarkozy must have been very convinced by what he heard and saw of Gebril.

Although winning the support of France was important, it would not be enough to convince the UN Security Council to install a no-fly zone over Libya. On 12 March, in a unique moment of decisiveness and consensus, the Arab League too asked for a no-fly zone. But to push this through, the support of the United States was needed. That was a problem. The US was surprised by the Arab League's demand, but had no appetite for another Arab war. Colum Lynch, a well known American journalist wrote that Susan Rice, US Ambassador to the UN, snapped to her French colleague who asked for support: "You are not going to drag us into your shitty war."[1]

Two days before the vote on Resolution 1973 on 17 March, 2011, Rice changed position and started actively trying to convince the other countries to endorse the resolution. On 15 March, Rice said: "We are discussing very seriously and leading efforts in the Council around a range of actions that we believe could be effective in protecting civilians – those include discussion of a no-fly zone. But the US view is that we need to be prepared to contemplate steps that include, but perhaps go beyond, a no-fly zone, as the situation on the ground has evolved, and as a no-fly zone has inherent limitations in terms of protection of civilians at immediate risk." What happened?

Lynch writes that "… the United States held a high-level teleconference with Obama's top national security team, including Rice and Secretary of State Hillary Clinton, who had just met with Arab leaders," and agreed to intervene. On 15 March, Clinton went to Cairo, where she met with Egyptian Foreign Minister El-Arabi and with Amr Moussa, Secretary-General of the Arab League, who explained why the Arab states were convinced about an intervention in Libya. It's no secret that Gaddafi was not especially liked by the other Arab leaders.

---

[1] Foreign Policy, 23 October 2012: http://blog.foreignpolicy.com/posts/2012/10/23/how_fair_is_obama_new_claim_that_the_us_lead_from_the_front_on_libya

However, few people know about the meeting Clinton had the day before, on 14 March, in Paris. She had to be there that day for the G8. It was most probably Sarkozy who convinced her to meet with Mahmud Gebril. After meeting with the French president, Gebril, Al-Issawi and Zeidan had taken the train to Brussels. Gebril quickly had to come back to Paris for probably the most important mission of his life: convincing the United States to support the UN resolution that would allow the installation of a no-fly zone in Libya. Clinton and Gebril met for 45 minutes. After the meeting, however, no declaration was given and no information was leaked, which is usually an indication that something important happened.

The rest of the story we know well. The Security Council adopted Resolution 1973 after intensive lobbying by France, the UK and the US. At the beginning of the meeting of those who had agreed to participate in the no-fly zone, France immediately sent fighter jets to Benghazi. Not less than 16 miles of military vehicles, full of soldiers and mercenaries loyal to Gaddafi, were at the gates of Benghazi. Some of had already entered the city. Their goal was simple: erase Benghazi, rape as many women (and men) as possible, kill everyone and destroy every building... executing Muamar Gaddafi's warning: "We will find you, wherever you are."

The new Political Isolation Law prevents Mahmud Gebril from becoming even a Member of Parliament. But this is not only about Gebril. It's about all those courageous Libyans who defected as soon as they could, as well as so many Libyans who gave and risked their lives for a better Libya. They are the ones who made the revolution succeed. Moreover, they are probably the best placed to rebuild the country destroyed by a Gaddafi past. It seems the Political Isolation Law might destroy the future of Libya as well.

TURKEY
Reflections from September 2011 to June 2013

Turkey was not meant to be part of my mission to the Arab world. However, very soon it became clear that *not* following Turkey would be a mistake. There are many historical ties between Turkey and the Arab world. And since Ahmet Davutoğlu became minister of foreign affairs, Turkey's foreign policy also began to focus on the Arab world again. His policy of 'no problems with our neighbours' has a strong neo-Ottoman smell. Let us not forget that for 400 years (16th to 20th century), most countries in the Arab world of today were part of the Ottoman Empire in one way or another.

Frustrated by the negotiations with the European Union, Prime Minister Erdoğan started to focus more on his ideological friends in the Arab world: the Muslim Brotherhood. This remained hidden to the West, however, until the protests on Taksim Square, Istanbul in May 2013. I was in Belgrade at the time and decided to take the first plane to Istanbul in order to see with my own eyes what was happening there. I was surprised to hear so many protestors complain about Erdoğan and the Islamic views he wants to impose.

One month later, it was again Erdoğan who reacted the most severely of the international community against the ousting of Morsi by the Egyptian army. From a Turkish point of view, this is more than understandable. Was Erdoğan's ideological predecessor, Necmettin Erbakan, not deposed by the army in 1997? Since then, Erdoğan's mission has been to never let this happen again.

After Mohamed Morsi was deposed, many Muslim Brothers fled to Istanbul. And it was Erdoğan who invented the sign with the four fingers as a symbol of protest against the massacre of Muslim Brothers in the Rabaa neighbourhood of Cairo. *Rabaa* means fourth in Arabic, while *arbaa* means four. Both Egypt and Turkey even recalled their ambassadors from each other's capitals.

Another reason why Turkey can't be ignored in any analysis of the events of the Arab Spring is its role in Syria. Davutoğlu's 'no problems with neighbours' policy had resulted in a good relationship between Ankara and Damascus. At the beginning of the Syrian Revolution, Erdoğan was even convinced he could change Bashar Al Assad's mind and stop the bloodshed. The moment it became clear that Erdoğan had no influence at all on Assad, he turned his policy around and started doing everything possible to make Assad fall. During a meeting behind closed doors among all governments supporting the Syrian opposition in Istanbul in the beginning of 2012, there was a vote on a military intervention in Syria: only Turkey and Qatar voted in favour.

As negotiations around Turkey's accession to the EU continue, it is crucial for the EU to follow closely what is happening there. Too often Turkey is considered 'too far from home'. However, the protests all over Turkey, and in Gezi Park in particular, show that a large section of the Turks want to make their country more, and not less, European. What Europe decides to do, or not do, with Turkey will shape the way the Arab world sees the European Union, its openness and diplomatic capabilities and thus its future.

1. Have we lost Turkey?
Published on *EU Observer*, 26 September 2011

A few nights ago, I was sitting on a roof terrace in Zamalek, Cairo, talking to one of the young leaders of the Tahrir Square revolution.[1]

With a beer in our left hand and a water pipe in the right, we talked about the revolution and how the April 6 Youth Movement had organised the protests day after day. These young people had started their protest movement already in 2008 – on 6 April, the 80th birthday of then leader Hosni Mubarak – with a huge strike all over Egypt.

During our discussion, he told an even more astonishing story. Along with 59 other young leaders from the April 6 Youth Movement, he was invited some weeks ago to visit Turkey. Not for tourism, though. They met with PM Erdoğan, with President Gul, with foreign minister Davutoğlu and many more.

These busy top politicians took their time, didn't rush and spoke freely of what their plans were for the future. Their message was that they want to create a new alliance between Turkey, Egypt and Iran. Turkey would invest substantially in Egypt, hoping for friendship and a big new market for its booming economy. What they plan to do with Iran is less clear. But it is obvious that these three countries are, in military and economic terms, by far the strongest in the region.

"By the way," he told me, "you in the West look differently at Iran than we do. For us, it is a strong country."

Of course, it is true that Turkey is becoming a leader in the region. To make it clear, Erdoğan recently visited Egypt, Libya and Tunisia – the three countries that have gotten rid of their dictators. He made a strong impression at a meeting of the Arab League, in Cairo in September 2011, when he said it was not an option but an obligation to support the Palestinians in their bid for statehood at the UN. He was greeted at the airport by crowds chanting, "Welcome, Erdoğan, Saladin!"

---

[1] See '4. From Twitter Revolution to Twitter Democracy' (30 January 2012) for a synopsis of the events of 25 January 2011.

The alliance could be a long-term goal. Could be. But a few days later, Turkish foreign minister Davutoğlu said in an interview[2] that he seeks an alliance with Egypt and that within the next two years, Turkey is going to invest no less than €4 billion in the country. Meanwhile, Europe is talking about one million.

In any case, my water pipe friend is not the only one happy with the idea – many Egyptians support it.

Whatever happens with the alliance in future, it is clear that Turkey has turned its head from the West to the East. Angry and humiliated because of the refusal to let them enter the EU (which has a religious dimension), they want to build their own union, based on secular Islamic principles.

Somehow I understand this. It is a lot nicer to be greeted as a hero in the East then as a beggar in the West. That is, after all, how the EU has treated them. An attitude we might soon regret.

---

2 *New York Times*, 18 September 2011: http://www.nytimes.com/2011/09/19/world/middleeast/turkey-predicts-partnership-with-egypt-as-regional-anchors.html?pagewanted=all

2. What would you do if you were Erdoğan?
Published in *The Parliament Magazine*, 6 February 2012

A few days ago, Rick Perry, a Republican candidate for the US presidency, said that Turkey was ruled by Islamic terrorists. That's why, he said, the US should think about kicking them out of NATO and why we should cut their foreign aid. This was followed by applause. I am speechless. This is the guy that succeeded George Bush as governor of Texas. Is this how the Republicans express gratitude towards Turkey for its crucial help in their war in Iraq?

It would be easy, however, for us Europeans to minimise this as one quote from one extreme American. However, in the past few years, we haven't been much better. We have seen individual politicians and rightist parties that have said that Islam is an inferior religion and that Islam and democracy don't match. And the list of those politicians, including Giscard d'Estaing (French president 1974 – 1981), who said that the EU is a Christian project in which Turkey could never fit, is too long to mention.

But as Turkish Prime Minister Recep Tayyip Erdoğan responded to d'Estaing, "These are emotions." So, let's go back to the facts. In 1963, Turkey became an associate member of the predecessor of the European Union. Turkey was one of the first non-founding members of the Council of Europe in 1949 and a founding member of the Organisation for Economic Cooperation and Development (OECD) and the Organisation for Security and Cooperation in Europe (OSCE). In 1987, Turkey applied for membership of the union, but this was blocked by Greece until 1999. In 2005, the negotiations finally started. A few years later, France and Germany both said they would never accept the entrance of Turkey. At the same time, the Turkish Cypriots accepted the peace plan of UN secretary-general Kofi Annan, while the Greek Cypriots rejected it – the result being that only the Greek side became a member of the EU. It are the same Greek Cypriots that are vetoing every single dossier in the EU negotiations with Turkey. Who would not be a bit frustrated?

At the same time of the elections in Egypt, Tunisia's new president is celebrating one year without dictatorship, Libya has begun developing a state from scratch and in Syria, people are confident they will topple

Assad. In these countries, almost all of the people are looking to Turkey. When Erdoğan visits, he is cheered by masses welcoming him as the new Saladin. The revolutionary youth of Egypt go to Turkey and are being treated like *pashas*. They come back to Egypt even more convinced Egypt's partner is Turkey, not the United States.

Since 1923 and the end of the Ottoman Empire, Turkey has tried to forget the East and look to the West. It has done its best to become accepted as a Western ally and a European country. Turkey's biggest trade partner by far is the EU. But if you looked at the imploding European economy compared to the Arab potential, what would you do? Although it's the right time to create partnerships around the Mediterranean, the EU and NATO are creating a new curtain, from the Strait of Gibraltar to the Bosphorus. Turkey lies on both sides of the Bosphorus. If you were Erdoğan, what would you do?

The EU can turn the tide and get Turkey back on board, but it will take a long and concerted effort to do so. And it is already clear that if we don't turn the tide, we will regret it. A lot.

3. Is Taksim the Turkish Tahrir? I thought not, until I came to Istanbul
Published on *Al-Monitor*, 3 June 2013

I was in Belgrade when I heard that people had started to demonstrate in Gezi park. Gezi park is one of the few green areas in the centre of Istanbul and is located on Taksim Square. The police interfered in a unnecessary brutal way in order to clear the park of protesters. As I felt this might be something big, I took the first plane on 30 May from Belgrade to Istanbul and went directly to Taksim Square. I spent the night on the square, where I saw similarities with what I had seen so many times on Tahrir Square in Cairo. At first, the following piece was received with mixed feelings in the European Parliament. Many thought it was highly exaggerated. That changed later on when Erdoğan reacted more and more in an authoritarian way. The reaction on the Turkish opposition side was very supportive. The very few media that wanted to show what was going on, called me for interviews. One of them, Hayat TV also asked me for help. The Turkish government decided to close the TV channel as they were broadcasting the protests on Taksim live. I published an open letter of Mustafa Kara, the broadcasting coordinator of Hayat TV, on my blog. To my surprise, it was read by a European media agency. They contacted the Turkish authorities. This saved Hayat TV from being closed down.

Turkey is not Egypt. Taksim is not Tahrir. That was my conviction when I arrived in Istanbul on 1 June, but when I entered Taksim Square, I was more than a little surprised. I did not expect so many people. I immediately felt a Tahrir vibe. The atmosphere was friendly, relaxed. Deep into the night, people began to collect the rubbish spontaneously.

The first person I approached answered without hesitation when I asked him what this was all about: "This is the same as the Arab Spring. We want the government, and certainly the prime minister, to listen to the people. But even better, it's time for him to go. You see how he controls the media? They pretend nothing is happening here."

A TV broadcasting van lay upside down, covered with graffiti. A girl shouted, "We are with thousands here, being beaten and attacked with tear gas, and on TV they talk about penguins and dolphins instead."

The protesters in Turkey are angry. Angry about the peaceful protesters at Gezi Park being attacked by the police with pepper spray, tear gas and water canons. Angry because of a law passed the preceding week that forbids the purchase of alcohol in shops after 10 pm. Angry about a new bridge in Istanbul being named after an Ottoman sultan responsible for the slaughter of 30,000 Alevis, who comprise roughly 15% of Turkey's population today. They are now also angry about the brutal way in which the police reacted to the Taksim and Gezi protesters. Several people told *Al-Monitor* that plainclothes police officers with iron bars had been seen destroying property. They were recognizable by their blue hats. An older man lamented, "Democratic states don't have tactics like this."

Despite the Tahrir feel of Taksim, one must of course acknowledge that the differences are substantial. Mubarak was a dictator, Recep Tayyip Erdoğan is an elected prime minister. In Turkey, there is freedom of speech, which was not the case in Egypt, Tunisia or Libya. Although some of the Turkish protesters were calling for Erdoğan to resign, it is doubtful, at this point at least, they really mean that. If the prime minister persists, however, in claiming that the protesters are terrorists or a bunch of losers being duped by the opposition, the calls for his resignation might quickly become serious.

It is clear that Taksim is not being controlled by dangerous people or by any of Turkey's political parties. A multitude of convictions and confessions are represented there. Some political parties have deliberately not taken part, as they cannot yet sense where all this will lead and do not want to be accused of inciting anarchy in case things get out of control. More important, it is not clear what exactly the protesters want. The events that have thus far transpired have been spontaneous reactions, without direction or guidance from anyone.

This spontaneity is the biggest problem for protesters in Taksim and across the country. It is also the biggest difference from Tahrir, where activists had been preparing the people for nonviolent action. In Egypt, there was an organization, the April 6 Youth Movement, and there was a strategy with a clear goal: removing President Hosni Mubarak from power using nonviolence. In short, in Tahrir Square, people knew exactly what they wanted and how to go about achieving it.

That is the weakness of the Turks of Taksim. There is no organization, which also means no control over people potentially ignoring and therefore damaging the nonviolent nature of the protests. If there is no organization, there is also no strategy. The thousands of people know exactly what they are angry about, but not what they collectively want to achieve. In this respect, Taksim more resembles Tunisia than Egypt. The Tunisian revolution was sparked by a single incident, the self-immolation by a street vendor, that brought to the surface a common anger that led to a spontaneous, but no-less-determined, call for justice, bread and freedom. As everyone knows, it also led to the fall of the dictatorship of Zine el-Abidine Ben Ali.

There is no dictatorship in Turkey. Rather, what people in the streets are angry about is what Alexis de Tocqueville called the "tyranny of the majority." No one questions the voting majorities that Erdoğan and his Justice and Development Party have assembled in fair elections, but they do not accept this majority forcing its agenda on the minority simply because it can. It certainly angers them that the media is apparently part of this majority or has been cowed by it, lacking the courage to report protests and dissatisfaction by large numbers of citizens. In the end, however, democracy demands the protection of the minority from the majority. This is why the Turkish democratically elected prime minister should reconsider his instinctively hostile response to democratic mass protests.

People in every Arab Spring country had one thing in common: they were protesting and even risking their lives for more freedom and more democracy. They wanted to be listened to, not dictated to by an authority – whether a king, dictator or majority – trying to tell them what was best for them. Thus, if one considers Tahrir Square the symbol of the revolution in Egypt, Taksim Square is clearly not the same for Turkey. If one, however, considers Tahrir the symbol of the peoples of the Middle East and North Africa demanding more freedom and democracy, then without a doubt, Taksim is the Turkish Tahrir.

4. Judy asks: is Turkey becoming more Western or less?
Published on Judy Dempsey's *Strategic Europe*, Carnegie Endowment for International Peace, 12 June 2013

Every week on Strategic Europe, *leading international affairs experts answer a new question from editor in chief Judy Dempsey on the foreign and security policy challenges shaping Europe's role in the world.*

Koert Debeuf, Representative of the European Parliament's Alliance of Liberals and Democrats for Europe

"Since the Justice and Development Party (AKP) came to power a decade ago, Turkey has definitely become more Western.

However, for a few years it has been sliding away from the West again. One of the reasons for this is the country's relationship with the EU. Prime Minister Recep Tayyip Erdoğan and the AKP seem to have replaced their European dream with an Ottoman dream. A short chronology explains why.

1. April 2004: Referendum on the Annan Plan for resolving the Cyprus dispute. Turkish Cypriots vote in favor, Greek Cypriots against.
2. May 2004: Greek-speaking Cyprus becomes a member of the EU. It starts to block the opening of some chapters of Turkey's EU accession negotiations.
3. December 2004: The EU decides to start accession negotiations with Turkey.
4. October 2005: EU accession talks with Turkey begin.
5. November 2005: Angela Merkel is elected as German chancellor. She openly opposes Turkey's EU accession.
6. May 2007: Nicolas Sarkozy is elected president of France. He too opposes Turkish EU membership.
7. May 2010: Merkel rules out the possibility of Turkey becoming an EU member.

8. September 2010: In a referendum, 60 percent of Turks vote in favor of a more European constitution.
9. December 2010: The Arab Spring starts.
10. October 2011: Elections in Tunisia lead to a victory for Islamist parties.

These developments have led an increasing number of frustrated Turks to believe that their country will never be a full EU member. It is therefore no wonder that, since 2010, the AKP – and more specifically Turkey's Foreign Minister Ahmet Davutoğlu – has developed a new strategy based more on Islam than on Western ideals.

Europe created Turkey's current problem and can still solve it. But it has no time to lose."

JORDAN
Some reflections

Jordan is one of the few countries in which the Arab Revolution seems to have changed nothing. It, above all others, fuels the theory that kingdoms are surviving while civil dictatorships have fallen. And indeed, the kings of Morocco, Jordan and Saudi Arabia, and the sultans and emirs of the smaller Gulf States are still in place, while the presidents of Tunisia, Egypt, Libya and Yemen were forced to resign. In the case of the Gulf States, it is clear that money has played an important role: the rulers have enough means to 'buy off' their citizens. People there feared they might lose a lot by risking a revolution. In the case of Morocco and Jordan, it has certainly helped the leadership that both kings' bloodlines go back to the family of the Prophet Mohamed.

Nevertheless, people in Jordan did protest. That I could witness the last time I visited Jordan, in November 2012. Jordanians were angry that the promised economical and political reforms had not been realized. However, shortly after, all protests suddenly stopped. And never made a comeback. Why? Just after my visit to Jordan, on 22 November 2012, Egypt's president, Mohamed Morsi, issued his extraordinary constitutional decree[1] in which he took all power, sidelining the Egyptian judiciary and pushing through the constitution.

It is hard to overestimate the impact of Morsi's mini-coup in the Arab world. Most Arabs were shocked to see the Muslim Brothers abusing their power to enforce their will onto the people. And what citizens all over the Arab world have noticed, is that more democracy meant more power for the Muslim Brotherhood. They were, after all, the best organized in every single Arab country, which enabled them to win almost every election.

When President Morsi issued his decree, the Muslim Brothers of Syria and Tunisia (Ennahda) declared that they were different from their Egyptian counterparts and that they would never follow the same path. The people weren't convinced. Soon after the Morsi decree, Ennahda in Tunisia got into trouble, losing support in the governement, while the Muslim Brotherhood in Syria lost its key position in the Syrian Opposition Council. And the events in Egypt also halted political reform in Gulf States like the United Arab Emirates.

Jordanians realized that the political reform they wanted would benefit only the Muslim Brotherhood, the most organized party in the country. Fearing this consequence, they stopped taking to the streets. As

---

[1] See '12. Egypt and the psychology of dictatorship: an outsider's perspective' (25 November 2012)

few Western analysts are following Jordan, few of us realized what was going on. I only realized the psychological impact of Morsi's mini-coup on Jordan after I had finished the following report to the ALDE group.

1. And revolution again in Jordan
ALDE Report, 29 November 2012

Last week, I was in Amman to investigate the protests in Jordan. I went to one of the street demonstrations. It was an interesting summary of what is going on. People shouted slogans against the rise of oil prices (+53%, due to the cut in subsidies) and demanded freedom and democracy. When one man shouted, "*Asshab yurit eskat el nizam*" ("the people ask for the end of the regime"), those around him asked him to shut up. However, this is nonetheless the first time that people on the street are shouting at the King: reform or leave. Why?

First of all, it's economics. Jordan is not doing well. As a result of the Arab Spring, tourism has dropped significantly. A taxi driver explained to me that he needs to pay 25 Jordanian dinar per day to rent his car; that he needs to drive around a lot to find clients, which costs him about 20 dinars in gas oil; and that at the end of the day he earns only 5 to (a maximum of) 10 dinars. Taking into consideration that one dinar is equal to one euro, and that Jordanian living standards are more or less on par with those of Europe, one can understand people taking to the streets if gas oil prices rise more than 50%.

The second reason is politics. Jordan has a difficult history with democracy. In 1956, the late King Hussein organized the first multi-party election, with a government appointed by the parliament. However, one year later, he dissolved the parliament, as it would have had too many links to the Baathists in Syria and Iraq. When Hussein's cousin, the Hashemite king of Iraq, was toppled (and assassinated) by the Baathists, Hussein banned all political parties. In 1984, Hussein reinstalled the parliament of 1957! For those MPs who had passed away in the meantime, new elections were held. After the West Bank became an own entity in 1988, and Jordan no longer had any responsibilities for it, Hussein organised (in 1989) the first real elections since 1957. In 1990, the ban on parties was lifted. The voting system was, as is normal: for every eligible seat in a district, the voter has one vote. However, this system appeared to be 'too democratic', as the MB and other opposition groups were too well represented in the parliament. That is why, in 1993, Hussein changed the system towards one man, one vote (but for several seats). The consequence is that – as everyone knows in Jordan – people give their first vote to the candidate of their tribe or family. So, by limiting the number of votes to one, parliament was almost only filled with tribal people, loyal to the King.

After the unrest in 2011, the King promised reform. In reality, this reform would be very difficult. A national dialogue was organised. The MB refused to participate. As the MB is the only real party in Jordan, the Court is reluctant to open up the system. But King Abdallah had another idea: creating parties that could compete with the MB. Of course, if an entire system is built on keeping parties out of parliament, who would be motivated to create a party? Nevertheless, former prime minister Khasawneh kept dialogue open with the MB and found a compromise: citizens would have three votes; two for the district candidates and one for a national party list. The Court blocked his solution, he resigned, and the current government went back to the old system of one man, one vote. Except that for 27/150 seats there will be a national list, to be elected proportionally. MB finds this percentage ridiculously low and therefore refuses to participate in the elections.

More than half of the Jordanian population is Palestinian. They are mainly 'organised' according to the city in Palestine they fled. The Jordanians are 'organised' by (Bedouin) tribes or by families. In general, people expect from their tribe/family/group not protection but mainly services. Members of Parliament are in fact the 'legislative' services arm of one family/tribe/group, which makes politics a mainly service-driven thing. The disadvantage is that people have a very low estimation of politics. In fact, there are two systems in Jordan: one feudal system and one official (state) system, both headed by the King. And depending on what you need as a Jordanian you turn to the system that can best provide for that need. Everyone does want change, but at the same time, they see the King as the only guarantee for the unity of the country. Civil war between Palestinians and Jordanians is everyone's nightmare. The memory of Black Saturday, that day in 1979 when the Jordanian army massacred revolting Palestinians, remains. The Palestinians do see the King as their protector, which is the reason that they haven't joined any protests. But that might change.

King Abdallah is making the same mistake as all the other dictators in the region. He thinks he is popular enough to keep things as they are. Most surprisingly, after five months, President Morsi still thinks the same.

Both are convinced that the majority backs them and that they just have to hold on until the storm passes. Yet every day there are protests all over Jordan, in Egypt, in Bahrain, in Kuwait, by people who demand freedom, democracy and justice.

LEBANON
Some reflections[1]

---

[1] Although I didn't publish any articles on Lebanon during the Arab Revolution, I found it impossible not to include some reflections on Lebanese politics in this book. Morocco, however, does not have a dedicated chapter as I have not yet managed to visit the country. Although I visited Palestine three times in the past three years, I have chosen not to include Palestine in this book as the problem of Palestine/Israel goes far beyond the subject of the Arab Revolution.

Lebanon was in fact the first Arab country that I visited. I spent my holidays there, with my family, in the summer of 2008. I was electrified. For someone interested in ancient history, Lebanon – with its Phoenician, Greek and Roman archeological sites – is paradise. Equally fascinating is the country's diversity: Maronite Christian, Armenian, Greek Orthodox and Catholic churches; Shia, Sunni and Druze mosques; and a nightlife that made you forget all about these differences as people of all kinds of beliefs share the same table.

Lebanese politics is based on an equilibrium between confessions. In parliament, half of the seats are reserved for Christians, the other half for Muslims (64 seats each). The Christian seats are divided among Maronites (34), Greek Orthodox (14), Greek Catholics (8), Armenian Orthodox (5), Armenian Catholics (1), Protestants (1) and other Christians (1). The Muslim seats are divided among Sunni (27), Shia (27), Druze (8) and Alevie (2). The president of Lebanon must be a Maronite Christian, the prime minister a Sunni Muslim and the speaker of the Parliament a Shia Muslim. This complicated system is intended to keep all ethnic groups happy.

Nevertheless, the scars of the civil war (1975 – 1990) are noticeable on almost every corner of every street. They are reminders of the fragility of the Lebanese society. During and after the Lebanese civil war, Syria had extensive military and intelligence influence in Lebanon. Both Syrian president Hafez and his son Bashar Al Assad often dictated Lebanese politics. When prime minister Rafiq Hariri opposed Bashar Al Assad's wish to extend the term of Lebanon's then-president Emile Lahoud, the result was Hariri's assassination. The St George hotel in Beirut, severely damaged by the car bomb that killed Hariri on 14 February 2005, still has not been renovated. It remains a silent symbol of the vicious role the Syrian regime played, and continues to play, in Lebanon's politics.

On 8 March 2005, supporters of Syria's presence in Lebanon took to the streets. In response, all forces demanding Syria to leave Lebanon organized a march on 14 March. The numbers were high enough for this march to be called the 'Cedar Revolution'. As a result, the international community asked the Syrian government to clear out of Lebanon. That same year, Syrian troops left Lebanon after being present in the country for 29 years. Saad Hariri took over the leadership of his father's political party, the (largely Sunni) Future Movement, and of the new 14 March Coalition.

After an electoral victory in 2009, Saad Hariri became prime minister in a coalition government that included Hezbollah, the main pro-Syria movement in Lebanon. Hezbollah (which means 'party of Allah'), the party of the Lebanese Shia Muslims, is financed by Iran and has its own armed militias. The coalition between Hariri and Hezbollah surprised many observers, as it was widely assumed the latter were behind the assassination of Rafiq Hariri. When Saad pushed for cooperation with the Special Tribunal for Lebanon, which was investigating the murder of Hariri, Hezbollah withdrew its ministers from the government in 2011. Saad no longer had a majority and resigned as prime minister.

Fearing for his life, Saad fled Lebanon, where he was succeeded as party leader by his nephew, Ahmad Hariri. Ahmad was the first Arab leader I met during my ALDE mission. In August 2011, I visited the 14 March Coalition in Beirut in order to find out if he and his party would be interested in cooperating with the ALDE group. Ahmad explained that only Shia members of the Lebanese parliament had contact with parliaments of other countries; the speaker of parliament is always a Shia Muslim. This restriction on establishing direct international contacts (unless you were Shia) meant the 14 March Coalition was more than happy to work with ALDE.

On 11 September 2012, Ahmad visited the ALDE group in the European Parliament in Strasbourg. On the eleventh anniversary of 9/11 he explained how the political situation in Lebanon was deteriorating, mainly due to the fact that Hezbollah was actively participating in the Syrian conflict to support the Assad regime. He predicted more assassinations in Lebanon, even though all political parties were doing everything possible to avoid the Syrian war crossing the border and becoming a new Lebanese civil war.

Although the dark predictions of Ahmad Hariri became reality – dozens of people have been assassinated so far – there has, fortunately, not been a real Syrian spillover to Lebanon. The most important effect of the war in Syria is the refugees that have crossed the border. In January 2014, the number of refugees reached almost one million; Lebanon has only 4.4 million inhabitants. Obviously, this has put a lot of pressure on Lebanese society as prices of apartments went up while cost of labour went down.

On 16 January 2014, the Special Tribunal for Lebanon officially accused four members of Hezbollah of assassinating Rafiq Hariri and two leaders of Hezbollah of having planned it. On 22 January, Saad Hariri announced his return to Lebanon to prepare for the elections, planned in

November 2014. He also said he was prepared to form a new government with Hezbollah. At the same time, he blamed Bashar Al Assad for being behind the assassination of his father.[2] On 15 February, a new government was formed, with Tammam Salam as its prime minister. The composition of this government tells us a lot about the complexity of Lebanese politics. Of the 24 ministers, there are 5 Sunni Muslims, 5 Shia Muslims, 6 Maronite Christians, 2 Druze, 2 Greek Orthodox, 1 Armenian Orthodox, 1 Greek Catholic, 1 Catholic and 1 Protestant. It is unclear how long this government will last. But if there is one thing we can predict, then it is that Saad Hariri will become prime minister of Lebanon again in the months or years to come.

---

2   *Al Arabiya News*, 16 January 2014: http://english.alarabiya.net/en/News/middle-east/2014/01/16/Hariri-killing-trial-opens-with-Lebanon-violence-untamed-.html.

FURTHER REFLECTIONS ON THE EUROPEAN DISASTER IN THE ARAB WORLD

An important part of my mission over these three years of publishing was to contribute to better European foreign policy towards the Southern Neighbourhood. I tried to do this by writing reports about what I thought was happening in the Arab world and by helping to make sure that the ALDE group sent press releases with the right message at the right time. These press releases (which you can find on the ALDE website: www.alde.eu) were not only meant to put pressure on the European side, but also on the Arab side. Therefore I could use the network I had built on Twitter and Facebook to spread the messages of the ALDE group. A final way of trying to inspire (even a small) change in EU foreign policy towards the Arab world was by blogging.

The main goal behind most of my articles and blogs was to make Europe *move*. And – it must be said – the EU's policy on the Arab world was often disappointing. It's true that the Arab Revolution came, for Europe, at the worst possible moment. The European External Action Service, the European diplomatic corps, was still in its starting phase and, more significantly, the economic and financial crisis caused European member states to look inwards rather than outwards.

Perhaps worse is the fact that European institutions – not to say most Europeans – share a lack of knowledge of, and interest in, the Arab world. This lack of knowledge became abundantly clear during the EU-Egypt Task Force, the subject of the following piece. Lack of interest is the reason – at least in my opinion – we are making a mistake that will go down in the history books. As Guy Verhofstadt points out in the foreword of this book, the European Union is not even using its soft power to help spread European values like freedom, democracy and respect for human rights.

It is not too late to change that course. Indeed, it is high time we do.

1. EU-Egypt Task Force: the perfect misunderstanding
Published on *EU Observer*, 15 November 2012

"I didn't realize that you hate us," said European Commissioner Stefan Fühle after a two-hour discussion with Egyptian NGOs. It was the last meeting of the EU-Egypt Task Force. This Task Force had assembled 400 politicians and entrepreneurs for two days in Cairo in order to see how we could better cooperate. The meeting was high level. From the Egyptian side, the prime minister, foreign minister and many other ministers and members of the Shura Council (the Senate of Egypt) were present. From the European side, Lady Ashton was there, as were EU Commissioners Antonio Tajani and Stefan Fühle, and many foreign ministers and members of European Parliament.

The most important news from the Task Force was the announcement by the European Commission to support Egypt with no less than €5 billion. Not without conditions, though. Egypt had to comply with the conditions of the IMF, something Egyptians don't really like to hear. They have a collective historical aversion of foreign loans. It was King Mohamed Ali who took loans from Britain and France to build the newly independent Egypt into a European-style power in the first half of the 19th century. When he was unable to pay back the loans, Britain took half of the Egyptian ministries. It was only until the Suez crisis in 1956, more than a century later, that Egypt succeeded in kicking the foreign powers out and regained its independency. This historical fear, together with the feeling of humiliation – why can't we govern our own business in a proper way? – makes Egyptians both happy and unhappy about foreign support, certainly if it is conditional.

Conditions, that is what it is all about. When I visited Shafiq (then still Prime Minister) just after the revolution, he reminded us that we had supported Mubarak and we were not well placed to tell the Egyptians what to do. A few months later, we met with PM Sharaf and he told us the same thing. Guess what, this week PM Qandil and President Morsi sent the Europeans exactly the same message. And the Europeans, feeling guilty about the Mubarak era, back off – at least publicly – not realizing that by being silent they make the same mistake as they did with Mubarak. The most obvious example of this week was the incident with the civil society.

The Egyptian government had invited civil society (NGOs, human rights and development organisations) to participate in the EU-Egypt Task Force. A few days before the meeting, the government withdrew its invitation. The European Commission was not pleased and deliberated over what they could do. Either they could cancel the whole thing, but in their eyes that seemed exaggerated, or they could insist on meeting the civil society separate from the official programme. That's what they did.

So this is the core of the perfect mutual misunderstanding. The EU honestly thinks that as long as they listen to civil society and take their remarks seriously, everything is fine. A high-level European representative even suggested the civil society be grateful as the EU did organise a dinner with them. The Egyptian civil society was utterly shocked that they had been erased from the official delegation and sidelined to a dinner. Why? This is not only about pride. This is about the revolution itself. It was not the organisers of the Task Force who risked their lives on Tahrir Square. On the contrary, these are exactly the same people from 20 (some even 40) years ago. It was these guys who sidelined civil society under Mubarak and who repeated the same behaviour. As if the revolution never happened.

When European Commissioner for Neighbourhood Policy Stefan Fühle comes to explain during a dinner for the sidelined civil society that human rights and democratic conditions are included in the EU package, he should not be surprised when the attendees react sceptically and even angrily. Because if he is serious about these conditions, why did he allow the Egyptian government to sabotage the first opportunity in which his words could be applied? And this in the very week, one year later, that more than 40 youngsters were killed by police snipers in clashes in Mohamed Mahmud Street. Nevertheless, Mister Fühle, the Egyptians don't hate the EU. But they are frustrated and disillusioned. They had hoped for more. Much more. And frankly, they are right.

2. How the EU is losing its entire Neighbourhood
Published on *EU Observer*, 11 September 2013

Many Europeans were baffled when they saw the recent images from Kiev's Independence Square of, as it is now being called, the Euromaidan: hundreds of thousands of Ukranians taking to the streets, defying the cold and police warnings, to wave EU flags and to chant "Europe!"

How is this possible?

Not one EU citizen would even consider going to stand on a snowy square with a European flag in his hand to ask for more European integration or a bolder European foreign policy. No. The mood in the EU is one of scepticism, cynicism and indifference. The trend is one of scaling down and of being everything but ambitious.

The result is that the European Union is driving with the handbrake on. It does take measures, but these are always too little, and often too late, to solve the problem or meet the challenge. One example is the financial and economic crisis. Another is the Neighbourhood Policy, which is becoming an unprecedented disaster.

In November 2013 Ukraine broke off negotiations on its Association Agreement with the EU. Armenia did the same thing in September. Instead, it decided to join the Russian Eurasian Economic Community's 'Customs Union'. Ukraine appears to be following suit. The reality is that Russia bought them out.

A similar scenario is unfolding in the Union's Southern Neighbourhood. In the Arab world, the main player is not Russia but the Gulf countries, however. Since July, Egypt has turned its back on the EU and the United States, while receiving billions from Saudi Arabia, Kuwait and the Emirates. Jordan has a direct financial lifeline from Saudi Arabia. Qatar is playing a major role in Libya while Morocco is increasingly looking to the Gulf for a solution to its financial problems.

It is hard to overestimate what is happening. Talks about a customs union and a common currency in the Gulf have been going on for a long time without any progress. But this might change very soon. Just as European integration always moves faster when there is an external threat,

Gulf integration is moving faster because of the threat of Iran. This week, the Gulf countries decided to organise a common military command.

The Arab region fears that Iran is breaking free of its isolation. Every Sunni Muslim country is convinced that Iran, a Shia Muslim power, will do everything it can to further destabilise the region by supporting Shia Muslim protests. The fact that their old allies, the US and the EU, are the engines behind the new deal with Iran, makes them unreliable in the eyes of many Sunni leaders.

But the lack of any serious EU neighbourhood policy is probably most evident in Libya. It is the only Arab Spring country where the Muslim Brotherhood did not win the elections. The hopes of the ruling government were set on Europe. Libya needs a lot of support to build a proper security apparatus, to deal with demands for autonomy and to organise a genuine national dialogue in which reconciliation is top of the agenda.

What the EU is currently doing is far too little and the consequence is that Qatar is stepping in. It is supporting the Muslim Brotherhood in Libya. It is helping to push militias to threaten the government to adopt legislation like the Political Isolation Law[1] and a law that forbids interest on bank savings. Its goal is clear: preparing the ground for its own political puppets and its own Islamic banks. If you have both, you control the economy and the oil.

Many Europeans might not care about these regional struggles and shifting alliances. But many Egyptians, Libyans, Moroccans, Tunisians, Jordanians, Armenians, Georgians, Ukrainians and Azerbaijanis do care. This year, I heard from all of them that they had strongly hoped the EU would step up to the plate. Even in Baku, Azerbaijan, everyone is asking for the EU to be more present as they feel squeezed between an increasingly confident Russia and Iran. The people of these countries know well that the history of the European Union has been one of turning poor dictatorships into prosperous democracies.

Even those Europeans who are less interested in high ideals and the freedoms of other people, should think twice before they shrug their shoulders: a less stable neighbourhood means more illegal immigration. It also means the end of energy supply diversification, making the EU more dependent on the mood swings of Moscow and Riyadh.

---

1 See '2. The untold story of Libya's Mahmud Gebril' (18 May 2013)

These are crucial times for the European Union. In one year, it may lose the alliances it has tried to build up for decades. It is time to wake up and to respond quickly and firmly. EU institutions are preparing for elections and for a change of guard in almost every top position. Despite this, Europe cannot afford to let those hundreds of thousands of Ukrainians down. The outcome of the Ukrainian dilemma is going to determine how serious the EU is about spreading freedom and democracy. If it loses Ukraine, the EU might also lose its entire Eastern and Southern Neighbourhood. The world is watching…

Bibliography

Abdel-Malek, A., *La Pensée politique arabe contemporaine*, Saint-Amand, 1970.
Abou El Fadl, Kh., *The Great Theft. Wrestling Islam from the Extremists*, New York, 2005.
Al-Khalili, J., *The House of Wisdom. How Arabic Science Saved Ancient Knowledge and Gave us the Renaissance*, London, 2010.
Al-Khalili, J., *Pathfinders. The Golden Age of Arabic Science*, London, 2012.
Ansary, T., *Destiny Disrupted. A History of the World Through Islamic Eyes*, New York, 2009.
Arendt, H., *On Revolution*, New York, 1965.
Brinton, C., *The Anatomy of Revolution*, New York, 1965.
Coller, I., "Egypt and the French Revolution", in Desan, S. et al. (eds.), *The French Revolution in Global Perspective*, London, 2013.
De Cock, J., *Arabische Lente. Een reis tussen revolutie & fatwa*, Antwerpen, 2012.
Doyle, W., *France and the Age of Revolution. Regimes Old and New from Louis XVI to Napoleon Bonaparte*, London, 2013.
Esposito, J.L. and Mogahed, D., *Who Speaks for Islam. What a Billion Muslims Really Think*, New York, 2007.
Fisk, R., *The Great War for Civilisation. The Conquest of the Middle East*, London, 2005.
Goody, J., *Renaissances. The One or The Many?*, Cambridge, 2010.
Hazard, P., *La crise de la conscience européenne (1680-1715)*, Paris, 1935.
Hibbert, Ch., *The French Revolution*, London, 1982.
Houssein, T., *La traversée intérieure*, Paris, 1992.
Hunt, L., "The Global Financial Origins of 1789" in Desan, S. et al. (eds.), *The French Revolution in Global Perspective*, London, 2013.
Jainchill, A., "1685 and the French Revolution" in Desan, S. et al. (eds.), *The French Revolution in Global Perspective*, London, 2013.
Kant, I., *An Answer to the Question: 'What is Enlightenment'*, London, 2009.
Keane, J., *The Life and Death of Democracy*, London, 2009.
Kennedy, H., *The Great Arab Conquests. How the Spread of Islam Changed the World We Live In*, London, 2007.
Kung, H., *Der Islam; Geschichte, Gegenwart, Zukunf*, Munchen, 2004.
Kwass, M., "The Global Underground: Smuggling, Rebellion, and the Origins of the French Revolution" in Desan, S. et al. (eds.), *The French Revolution in Global Perspective*, London, 2013.
Lawrence, T.E., *Seven Pillars of Wisdom*, London, 1997.
Merriman, J., *A History of Modern Europe: From the Renaissance to the Age of Napoleon*, (vol. 1.), New York, 2009.

Mirkin, B., *Arab Human Development Report. Arab Spring: Demographics in a region in transition*, United Nations, New York, 2013.
Morgan, M.H., *Lost History. The Enduring Legacy of Muslim Scientists, Thinkers, and Artists*, Washington, 2007.
Morris, I., *Why the West rules – for now. The patterns of history and what they reveal about the future*, London, 2011.
Nasr, A.A., *My Islam. How Fundamentalism Stole My Mind – And Doubt Freed My Soul*, New York, 2013.
Nussbaum, M.C., *The New Religious Intolerance. Overcoming the Politics of Fear in an Anxious Age*, Cambridge, Massachusetss, 2012.
Osman, T., *Egypt on the brink. From the rise of Nasser to the fall of Mubarak*, New Haven – London, 2011.
Outram, D., *The Enlightenment*, Cambridge, 2013.
Roberts, M. and Eldrigde, A., *Planning the Night-time City*, London, 2009.
Rogan, E., *The Arabs. A History*, New York, 2009.
Said. E.W., *Orientalism*, London, 2003.
Spieler, M., "Abolition and Reenslavement in the Caribbean: the Revolution in French Guiana" in Desan, S. et al. (eds.), *The French Revolution in Global Perspective*, London, 2013.
Talbi, M., *Plaidoyer pour un islam moderne*, Tunis, 2006.
Toffler, A., *The Third Wave*, New York – Toronto – London – Sydney – Auckland, 1980.
Walton, Ch., "The Fall from Eden" in Desan, S. et al. (eds.), *The French Revolution in Global Perspective*, London, 2013.